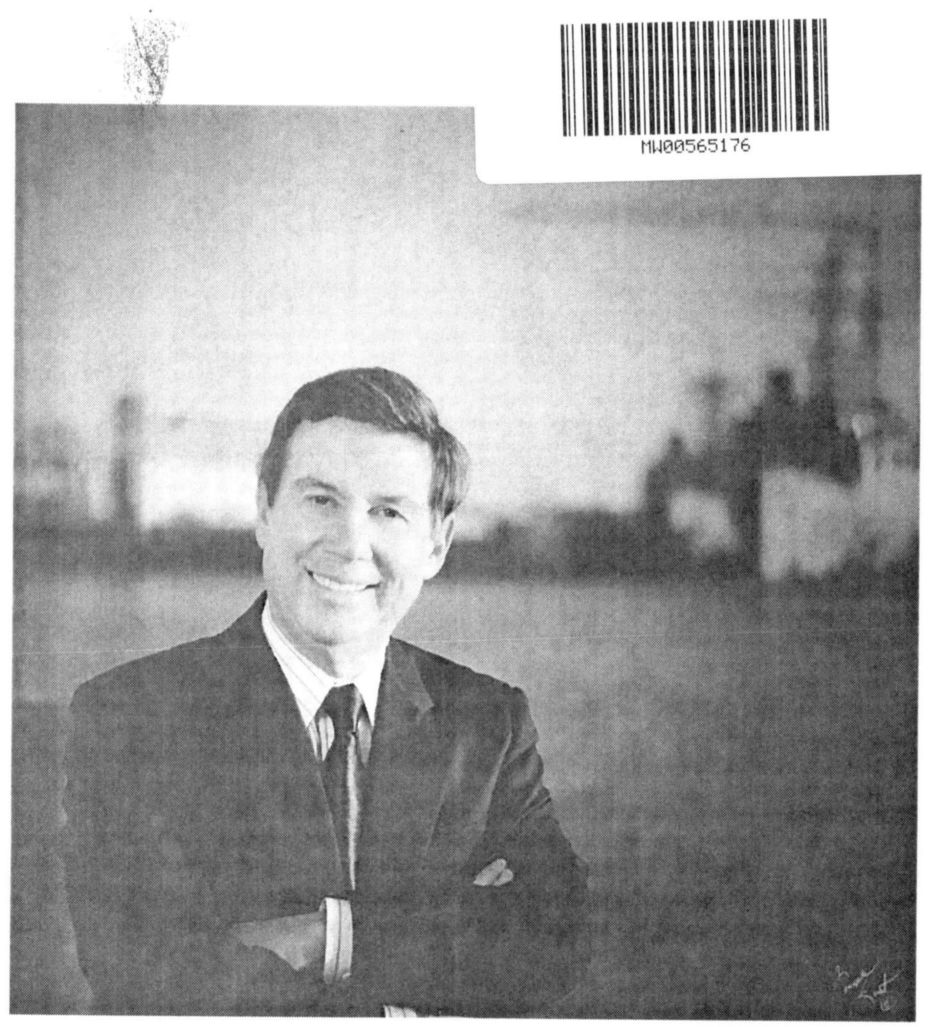

Building Shipwright Success on Life's Miracles

A Memoir by Richard A. Goldbach

Printed in the United States of America
2017 First Edition
10 9 8 7 6 5 4 3 2 1
Goldbach, Richard A.
Title: Building Shipwright Success on Life's Miracles
1. Metro Machine 2. Employee Stock Ownership Plan (ESOP) 3. Capitalism 4. Webb Institute 5. Leadership
6. Business 7. U.S. Navy 8. Department of Defense 9. Unites States Government

Paperback ISBN: 978-0-692-97227-4
Library of Congress Card Catalog: 2017916558

Cherry Grove Plantation, L.L.C.
1554 Cherry Grove Rd. North
Suffolk, VA 23432

www. shipwrightsuccess.com

Praises for Shipwright Success...

"I've finished your book. I need to write you about it here, but I don't think I'm up to the job of conveying how overwhelmingly impressive and inspiring it is on so many levels, so many dimensions...

It is intensely private, insightful, and far-reaching. It is humbling to learn better the part I played in a truly great life that touched and helped and saved so many people. I understand it as the love story you intended it to be.

It is also a testament to something like karma or God's will or the golden rule, in that you worked so hard in such adversity to boldly act where others would or could not--and did so repeatedly throughout your life to date...and to be rightly rewarded with so many unique accomplishments and the earned admiration and love of so many people, first among whom is Janet of course. I am so happy to know the two of you have each other, as you deserve, as lifelong soulmates. She, like you, is an amazing person, which I realize all the more with the many loving and challenging times you describe in your happy journey together.

Thank you for including me in your life and in your beautiful memoir. If I could adequately explain what you have meant to me, it would be in glowing eloquent terms that would warm your heart, as you have warmed mine, at so many points over the years.

I hope we have many more years to mutually enjoy the challenges and joys of life."

With love and admiration,
Ken Cooper,

"When I asked if I might read the manuscript of your memoir prior to printing I had no idea of the adventure I was about to experience. Having known each other since our early college days, more than 62 years and all of our adult lives, having stayed at each other's homes, and having interacted numerous times on social and professional occasions throughout our respective careers, I thought I knew you quite well. As I began reading your manuscript I soon realized that there were many aspects of Richard A. Goldbach that I knew nothing about. Once I began reading it was difficult to put the book down. I read it in two sittings, captivated by stories that revealed an extraordinary life, by any measure, a life well lived. Although I knew some of the stories, I had no idea of the scope and breadth of your contributions and life-long commitment to the betterment of those whose lives you touched.

Your commitments to your professional life, extraordinary as they are, have been only one part of a multi-faceted voyage, rich in personal initiatives at so many levels, in caring for the betterment of people in your community, throughout the spectrum of one on one interactions, family, fellow workers, to the broadest scope of neighborhood, industry, and all aspects of civic involvement. Perhaps the most moving aspect of this inspiring and wonderful story is that so much of it has been done quietly but with a consistency of determination in the beliefs that you hold so strongly. That I am not alone in my admiration is well documented in the many accolades cited in your book. I commend you for writing a fascinating "tale of tales." I know that it will inspire all who read it.

Bravo, my friend, bravo!"
Joe Cuneo

"Thank you for allowing me to be one of the first readers of your book. I'm grateful you chose me, and to say I enjoyed it would truly be an understatement. After knowing you for most of my adult life, along with hearing some of the stories of your past, I was hoping for a "feel good" book, and I was definitely not disappointed. Once I started reading, I found myself wanting to finish the entire book before I put it down for even the first time.

The feelings I experienced ranged from intrigue, to amazement, to being extremely proud, (of you along with being a part of it), and very emotional at times. At one point I remember feeling the same way I did while watching Rocky II, when Rocky won the fight and yelled " yo Adrien I did it". Maybe to some degree you were like the underdog that never gave up, and won at the end of the last round. Maybe its because you worked so hard for others instead of just yourself. One thing for sure, is that Metro's employee ownership journey was truly one of Life's Miracles that will always be one of my most treasured memories.

We've had so many great times together, and reading your book has rekindled so many fond memories. I also really enjoyed reading some of the stories of your past, especially ones that I had heard of, but not at the intimate level that you share them in the book. Everyone has struggles in life, and yours were more difficult than many others, However, reading through them was both heartwarming, and encouraging.

Once again, I appreciate the opportunity to be one of the first readers, and I reflect on some of the Life's Miracles you describe frequently. Our working relationship along with our friendship has, and always will be very special to me. I think it's remarkable how you are able to put these experience to paper in a way that captures the emotions so intensely."

John Strem

Since before Recorded History,
the Navies of all Great Nations
have employed Shipwrights
to do the work of the Shipyards
that have Built and Repaired
the Warships they used to defend
their shores and project power.

Dedication

These memories are dedicated to Janet, Henry, John and all the Metro Machine employee-owners who every day did the difficult and important things our Nation needed and trusted us to do well. Always working with bright, hard-working, honest, friendly and enthusiastic folks was sure fun for me. I looked forward to it every morning as I drove through the Metro Machine gate. I hope you did too!

I know there were some days you had to hold your breath. For what it's worth, I was probably doing the same thing on those days. The courage I derived from your hanging in with me on those days was indispensable to our accomplishments during the 25 years of what was U.S. capitalism's best-ever example of real employee ownership.

The way I got through the most difficult days was by assuring myself that I was doing my best to meet my obligations to you, never being certain until 2011 that my best was going to be good enough.

It was the biggest thrill of my lifetime when we succeeded and I could finally believe it.

Table of Contents

Prologue

The story behind the story of *Building Shipwright Success on Life's Miracles* is that our encounters with people and situations accumulate and mold us into being what we are at every instant of life. This means that we are perpetually evolving into a different being, no matter how we will it otherwise.

These tales describe the life of an Engineer who had the best ringside seat during the six-decade construction, conversion, repair and environmentally compliant disposal of the U.S. Navy ships which replaced World War II aircraft carriers, submarines, cruisers, destroyers, frigates, amphibious ships and auxiliary ships.

They also detail how the Engineer earned this seat by:

- Working in shipyards for almost 57 years
- Being employed building, converting, repairing and dismantling U.S. Navy ships in 10 separate shipyards, four of which he managed;
- Working on board all of the U.S Navy's ship types;
- Working in shipyard management offices, design drawing rooms, fabrication shops, production shops, on building ways and outfitting piers as well as in drydocks;
- Having the 34-years service as shipyard CEO which culminated in his shipyard career being longer than that of any other in the industry; and
- Receiving more shipyard patents issued than any other predecessor.

The turning-point in the Engineer's life and the lives of many others was the day in 1975 when the Engineer was demoted while working for Ingalls Shipbuilding in Mississippi.

Coincidentally, the turning point in the life of another, who was a self-made Working Man in Virginia, was when he used his $10,000 life savings to found a shipyard company located one thousand miles away from the Engineer and from Ingalls.

A Virginia lawyer named Bingo Stant introduced the Engineer to the Working Man. The Working Man's shipyard company was in great difficulty in 1977 because it had no shipyard work, and the Navy stated his company would not get more work in the future.

That Virginia company and its workers comprised the life's work of the Working Man. He considered the company's workers to be his best friends.

In 1977, the Working Man trusted the Engineer to manage both his life's work and his best friends. As he did, he gave the Engineer an opportunity to achieve the goal that the Engineer most hoped to achieve. That goal was to become the most accomplished shipwright of his time.

Thirty-four years later, the Engineer believed he had achieved his goal. As he did, he financially rewarded the Working Man and his friends beyond their expectations. The Working Man's stock in the shipyard was purchased for $20 million in 1987. In 2011, the 400 workers of the shipyard were paid $165 million for company stock they had been given after 1987.

Henry Swanner, founder of Metro Machine Corporation in Norfolk, Virginia, was the Working Man. I was the Engineer.

The method I used to achieve personal and Metro Machine success employed all the incentives for working hard and doing good work, supposedly embodied in capitalism. In fact, the method I used had an additional incentive over traditional capitalism; workers received all of the financial benefit of shipyard success.

The method was called an Employee Stock Ownership Plan (ESOP). For 25 years, this ESOP made Metro Machine's more than 400 workers the most highly compensated shipwrights in the Nation. During that period, the shipyard remained very competitive in every way.

As the shipyard remained competitive, it met all requirements of its Navy contracts in a superb manner. The average Metro Machine performance fee scores awarded by the Navy during the years of Metro

Machine employee ownership were "Outstanding." As it performed in an outstanding manner, Metro Machine proved that permitting its workers to retain a fair share of the business profits they helped create, enabled them to live securely in a global economy.

There is one unique trait that I have always had which ultimately would have the greatest influence on my success managing shipyards. That trait is my thorough enjoyment of figuring out better ways to do things, especially finding ways to benefit others, rather than finding ways to benefit myself. As a youngster, I was sincere when I recited the Scout Law, "On my honor as a scout I will help other people at all times."

My most productive idea was creating employee ownership of Metro Machine and managing it to success. Knowing how that idea had ultimately brought fulfillment to Metro Machine workers is the satisfaction of my life.

In addition to my ability to make both technology and life better for the workers, I think another reason for the success I enjoyed was my being an engineer competing against business-oriented shipyard CEOs. Attending an engineering college, I never was taught how to exploit workers, as I observed CEOs doing in other shipyards who had business education and experience.

On the 12th of July, 1958, I was certified as an Engineer by one of the most respected Engineering colleges in the land. I had no idea in 1958 that most of my future efforts would be used to make life better for my company's workers, while competing with others, with different educational backgrounds that pursued their own success by exploiting the vulnerabilities of their workers.

The skills needed to compete with those who exploit workers are neither taught nor even mentioned in engineering colleges. The three shipyard mentors I emulated included two engineers and one working man. All three had great respect for skilled shipwrights and did not exploit them.

Although worker exploitation has always been socially acceptable, I have never practiced it and firmly believe that it is always wrong and unfair. I believe worker exploitation poses a great, if not the greatest long-term threat, to business in America. This exploitation of workers provides benefits to investors that are far in excess of their needs and far in excess of their fair share of America's bounty. It weakens America, as it destroys the workforce that is America.

Instead, I used the respectful way Metro Machine treated its workers, its workplace equality and its racial harmony as a competitive advantage. How can a company whose workers dread coming to work in the morning ever beat a company whose workers look forward to coming to work?

I disagree with the belief that American investors deserve to receive much more of the American bounty than the American workers themselves, based upon the premise that their work requires them to be smarter than the American workers. My first-hand experience convinces me it is just as intellectually demanding to be an expert shipwright, as it is to be an expert investment banker or an expert accountant.

I believe the overwhelming problem causing the social strife that exists in America today is lack of respect for workers and lack of due consideration for the economic needs of workers and their families. I believe this disregard enables a few strategically placed American white collar workers to exploit a multitude of America's highly skilled workers.

Unlike that of most other nations, America's bounty had been intended to benefit all of its citizens, including its workers, when America was established by its Founding Fathers. Although America was supposed to be a just place for all its citizens, like those of most other nations, America's workers have been exploited for the benefit of better-positioned fellow citizens during the advance of the global economy.

The inequitable allocation of America's bounty between those who control America's wealth and those who do America's work has been hidden in plain view for over a century. That is because most American workers have historically been paid enough to live on and most American workers were satisfied with that situation.

As the global economy advanced, fewer and fewer American workers could live on their paycheck income alone. This was in part, because the global economy increasingly resulted in export of some or all of the labor content of goods formerly manufactured entirely by

American workers.

In addition, the global economy increasingly exported new American worker jobs capable of being accomplished abroad by using the Internet. This included a high percentage of newly created American jobs associated with information and communication systems.

Finally, the global economy increasingly imported foreign workers to perform jobs that would otherwise have been performed by American workers. It did this by Government and industry exploiting relaxed immigration rules and enforcement of those rules.

This is hardly the first time that workers of a great power have been displaced by workers of dominated nations. This pattern of worker displacement has been an integral part of the rise and fall of all great powers, including Rome. So far, there has been no great power that has been able to reverse these economic trends without first collapsing.

I fear that too many American citizens benefit from the exploitation of America's workers for this trend to be reversed. To have an outcome different from history, America must come up with a new idea to enable its workers to be financially and physically secure in the global economy. This global economy will, almost certainly, exist as long as the world human population keeps increasing.

The Government has addressed the American worker hardship resulting from this exploitation by increasing Government entitlement expenditures funded by increased taxes. Decreased citizen earned income, increased entitlement expenditures wages, and increased taxes, then led to the Government having greater power over all its citizens.

Compensation using entitlements will never provide the positive incentive to American workers that earned income provides. That is because entitlements, by their nature, do not offer any incentives that encourage workers with latent skills to work harder and more smartly. Thus, compensation by entitlements is evenly distributed, irrespective of how hard or how smartly the workers are performing.

All evidence indicates that American worker salaries, including benefits, will continue to be severely constrained by the global economy. Only by sharing company financial success with workers in some other way will workers, presently lacking opportunity to live up to their potential, be able to afford making their way back into the workplace.

Sharing the profits of American industry through American worker ownership is the only other proven way to secure working Americans and America itself. Experience with employee ownership by Metro Machine and other companies proves that employee ownership can enable America's workers to receive their fair share of America's bounty.

The result of workers believing they have no opportunity to perform a task that uses their human potential and no chance of receiving a fair share of their nation's bounty, is clearly predictable from history. If you are ready for a chilling example of what might happen, you might revisit the occupation of Vienna by Hitler and the Nazis 80 years ago.

That terrifying occupation provides a way of predicting where today's American worker unrest can lead. When workers and their families become convinced that they are unable to live a financially and physically secure life, they will sometimes irrationally follow charismatic, but dangerous leaders. Some of these leaders might convince those frustrated workers to forcefully achieve a different balance of wealth. One doesn't have to go back to Vienna. This is happening now on the streets of America's cities.

Building Shipwright Success on Life's Miracles describes how Metro Machine's employee-owners came to trust that their ownership of their American company enabled them to live the secure and fulfilled life they believed they had earned.

Our elected legislators got something right when they enacted the ESOP legislation from which Metro Machine workers and the Navy benefited. We need to more urgently utilize that legislation, like Metro Machine did, to make many more American workers secure again.

Shipyard Odyssey

On October 31,2011, I drove out of the Metro Machine shipyard gate in Norfolk, Virginia for the last time, having served as Chief Executive Officer (CEO) since April 3, 1977. Shipyard work had been my only employment since January 3, 1955, when I reported as a shipwright trainee at the Brooklyn, N.Y. Naval Shipyard. It was hard to believe that almost 57 years had gone by and it was now time to retire.

I still have a clear picture in my mind of the Webb Institute of Naval Architecture Freshmen classmates, Rob, Ron, Bill and Pete being with me on the morning of January 3, 1955, when the five of us entered through the Sands Street Gate of the Naval Shipyard. My mind was full of hopes for the future.

A ten-week work term at the Naval Shipyard was a regular part of the Freshman curriculum at Webb Institute of Naval Architecture in Glen Cove, Long Island. By the end of that term, I had learned a little bit about dozens of highly specialized shipwright skills and how they interacted with each other. However, the only skills in which I ever considered myself to be expert, were engineering and production management.

I always had to depend on shipwrights with other skills to perform the multitude of other shipbuilding tasks, just as they had to depend on me to perform my functions. Over the years, I came to believe that my task, while normally more unique than most, was no more essential than those of other shipwrights. I realized that, just as their performing their jobs well was necessary for me to succeed, my doing my job well was a prerequisite for each of them to succeed. I concluded that shipyards were people machines, and I wanted to always be a reliable part of one of those machines!

My detailed understanding of that fact grew during each of my years in shipbuilding and eventually become one of my most important and unique contributions to the shipyards for which I worked.

The Webb Institute of Naval Architecture, located on one of the estates of the famous Pratt family, had just been declared "The Toughest School in the U.S." by the Saturday Evening Post. The five of us plus eleven other classmates were scheduled to return from our Winter Work Period to our academic rigors at the Glen Cove Campus in twelve weeks.

I hoped to become a highly skilled engineer who the U.S. Navy would depend on, just as it depended on my father. I hoped to be quick-witted, forceful and strong, like my mother. I hoped I would have a demeanor people liked, like my favorite teacher, Naomi Laubach. I hoped to someday find a woman who would blend her life and dreams with mine.

Incredibly, the young lady of sixteen years who was to do that was living just four blocks away from the rundown Margaret Hotel top-floor apartment into which my classmates and I had just moved. Although I wouldn't know it until I returned to Webb Institute three months later, I walked past her apartment twice a day for the next 10 weeks. She lived on Hicks Street, while I lived on Columbia Heights. Her name was Janet Clinton. She was already a famous magic entertainer.

As Rob, Ron, Bill, Pete and I passed through the Sands Street Gate together each morning, Janet was walking to Packer Collegiate Institute on Joralemon Street where she was a sophomore. Packer was the finest private girl's school in New York City, hardly the place a "yard bird" from the Brooklyn Naval Shipyard bunking in the seedy Margaret Hotel would dare approach when looking for female companionship.

So, my blind date with Janet Clinton was to await my return to Glen Cove. When it occurred, I was astonished to discover in her an extraordinary combination of intellect, refinement, enthusiasm, joy, humor, righteousness and inner strength. Never before had I observed such a combination of qualities in a single person. However, I soon learned she looked for these same qualities in those she befriended. If I were ever to convince her to blend her dreams with mine, I would have to commit to an entire lifetime of improvement.

I found my way through Webb Institute. Over the years of working at various shipyards, I came to feel the same concerns for shipwrights, the shipyard industry, my Community and the Nation that William Webb, the 1889 founder of Webb Institute, had felt. I was ready to make a difference. My first job after graduation was at the Electric Boat shipyard in Groton, Connecticut where I witnessed the genius of Al Zeien, the extraordinary persistence of Lloyd Bergeson and the awesome leadership of Norman McIntyre. I wanted to adopt their excellent qualities to be part of my personal "tool kit."

I came to a crisis in my career after two decades in shipyards as I was publicly and unfairly demoted and drawn into an unwarranted criminal investigation of Ingalls Shipbuilding.

As I fought through that crisis, with indispensable support from my wife, Janet and my Dad, Frank, I met a man who was fighting his way through a surprisingly similar crisis. Over time, he became my business partner and friend for life and little by little, I discovered he shared the William Webb concerns for shipwrights and the U.S. Shipbuilding Industry that had become important to me. That man was Henry Swanner.

As I fought through the crisis of the investigation, I also encountered, against incredible odds, an MIT graduate named Ken Cooper. Working with him greatly magnified my management capabilities. Ken introduced me to the technology of Systems Dynamics and helped me learn to use that technology for predicting the future in shipyards. I used that ability to outsmart my shipyard competitors.

Without my thinking about it, all of the human characteristics I had come to admire in others during my first four decades on Earth combined to guide me. To my everlasting relief and delight, this guidance enabled me, and many others who joined me, not only to survive, but also to experience success during my last 34 years in shipbuilding.

I tend to attribute that 34-year success to human guidance alone. Yet, on five occasions, something essential to success occurred for which I have no explanation. Nor can I point to any scientific belief which I feel could explain them. But the ultimate success of Metro Machine was built as certainly on these unexplainable occurrences as it was on the thoughtful guidance of others.

The first of these used criminal investigations to lead Henry and me, with our complementing capabilities and needs, to each other.

The second, used an unfair demotion to lead me to the System Dynamics technology. This technology proved to be essential for survival, for it underpinned the success of the Metro Machine production process.

The third, led me to a rarely-used Reagan tax cut provision which funded the drydock equity payment which was absolutely necessary to acquire a drydock, also essential for survival.

The fourth, used a dream to structure Metro Machine's stock ownership as an Employee Stock Ownership Plan or ESOP which too proved to be essential for survival.

Finally, the fifth, used a message that came to me, an engineer. This message saved a pastor, who then changed the world around him.

In each of these instances, it seems that the right kind of intervention that was needed to build Metro Machine success had taken place. Other related events seem to suggest other critical interventions.

Between 1955 and 2011, the number of East Coast U.S. Navy shipyards operating large drydocks reduced from six to one. The number of U.S. East Coast private shipyards operating large drydocks reduced from twenty to seven.

Only one of the U.S. shipyards operating a large drydock in 2011 was a small business. Only one was 100% owned by its employees. That single small employee-owned shipyard was Metro Machine which, despite its small size and lack of investor backing, had a higher ship repair sales volume and profit in 2011 than any other shipyard in the U.S.

Metro Machine had a net worth of one million dollars in 1977 when I was named CEO. After Metro Machine became employee owned and it borrowed to purchase the stock of its founder for $20 million in 1986, Metro Machine had a negative net worth. Following 1986, Metro Machine reinvested all of its profits to provide employee-owner jobs. Metro Machine's capital investment in facility expansion and improvement between 1982 and 2011 was greater than any other individual U.S. repair shipyard.

When Metro Machine's buyer bought its stock on October 31, 2011 for $165 million, the buyer was amazed to find Metro Machine had no debt and no legal or contractual disputes. All Metro Machine stock was owned by the ESOP, which distributed its stock fairly among all of the approximately 400 company-employees. This fair distribution was done in accordance with a formula approved by and subject to annual audit by the U.S. Internal Revenue Service.

The $165 million distributed to all Metro Machine employee-owners after sale of all Metro Machine stock far exceeded employee-owner expectations. The employees hadn't paid a cent for the stock that was distributed to them. Instead, the amount of their distributions came from all Metro Machine profits after August 31, 1986 being used to purchase additional stock, which was then contributed to the Metro Machine ESOP. Being a 100% ESOP, all Metro Machine profits were legally exempt from income taxes.

Metro Machine, which paid prevailing union wages, also provided a medical plan to its employee-owners which was considered to be the best in the region by both those employee-owners and Tidewater, Virginia medical providers. This plan cost individual Metro Machine shipwrights only small co-pays. The provided medical care included employee and family dental care furnished by an on-site, full-time dentist, working efficiently. This dentist was retired from the Navy, and was capable of performing almost all dental procedures.

As Metro Machine provided its employee-owners with job security, retirement security, health security, a fair workplace and a safe workplace, it also supported its community by becoming the largest corporate supporter of Norfolk inner-city causes, including elementary school reading programs, Boys and Girls Clubs and the Senior Citizen Center.

As Metro Machine provided for the needs of its employees and Community, it also served its Country as it became highly respected by NAVSEA (Naval Sea Systems Command), DCAA (Defense Contract Audit Agency), EEOC (Employee Equal Opportunity Commission), EPA (Environmental Protection Administration), DOL (Department of Labor) and OSHA (Occupational Safety and Health Administration), which constitute all the federal agencies U.S. shipyards must satisfy.

As Metro Machine provided for needs of its employees, its community and the U.S Navy, I served the City of Norfolk as its Chamber of Commerce Chairman, its National Maritime Center Chairman, its Tidewater Community College Board Member and its Boy Scout District Chairman.

While serving the City of Norfolk, I also served the Norfolk region ship repair industry as the founding President of the Tidewater Maritime Training Institute and the founding President of the South Tidewater Association of Ship Repairers.

How was this remarkable outcome accomplished in today's corporate world, especially when management and stockholders are routinely presumed to be motivated by greed?

First, all the stockholders were employees and all the employees were stockholders.

Second, the company was managed for the primary benefit of the employee-stockholders, not the management. I never made a Metro Machine senior management decision which benefited senior managers but hurt employee-owners.

Third, as sole ESOP Trustee, I voted all ESOP stock which gave me the latitude to make distant horizon decisions best for Metro Machine employee-owner long term interests. Since the ESOP owned all Metro Machine stock, I never had to make short-term decisions which favored passive investor selfish interests.

One example of distant horizon decisions I made included investing in the youth of the community so they would be better disciplined and more loyal workers when they came to work for Metro Machine in the future.

Only when company extinction was threatened, would I ever consider making a short-term decision which I knew could have harmful long-term consequences for employee-owners. Yet, if this occurred, I always knew that the decision I was making had the least long-term risk of available alternatives.

Finally, Metro Machine had extraordinary competitive advantages in the Navy ship repair industry because of the guidance of Al Zeien, Lloyd Bergeson and Norman McIntyre, and because, I, as CEO, had superior knowledge of and experience in the shipbuilding industry. In addition, and of great importance, I, as CEO, also had acquired a superior capability to look into the future.

This ability to look into the future was born in 1975 when, working for Litton Industries. I reluctantly inherited an extraordinary management problem of unprecedented complexity and national importance.

A seeming miracle occurred in the bookshelves of the American Management Association (AMA) Library in Manhattan, when, against all odds, I encountered the only person in the world capable of helping me find a solution to the problem I had inherited. The person was a then unknown MIT graduate named Ken Cooper.

The capability Ken employed was a little-known technology named Systems Dynamics, which was championed and taught by venerable MIT Sloan School professors Jay Forrester and Ed Roberts. Together, Ken and I would solve the riddle of the Litton problem, enabling Litton and the Navy to resolve a major dispute that had been inhibiting National Defense by delaying the entry of needed ships to the fleet.

As we helped resolve the Litton/Navy differences, Ken and I would also unveil solutions to similar future complex problems that we ourselves, confronted during the next three decades.

Thousands of Government workers, tens of thousands of shipwrights and millions of shipyard transactions were involved with the Litton problems needing resolution. Equitable resolution of this collection of individual differences required sorting through design impacts that had rippled through the interfaces of design, logistic support, construction and testing of 35 ships constructed over ten years.

When Ken Cooper's application of Systems Dynamics was teamed with my twenty years of shipyard manufacturing engineering experience with Al Zeien, Lloyd Bergeson and Norman McIntyre, it enabled Litton and the Navy to arrive at what both considered to be a fair and equitable compromise. Until this technological analysis was developed and employed, neither Litton, nor the Navy had been able or willing to admit there was merit in the other's assertions. The analysis proved, beyond the shadow of a doubt, that there was significant merit in the assertions of both Litton and the Navy .

This extraordinary unprecedented application of Systems Dynamics identified all the technical aspects of ship design, construction and testing; identified the most important principles of complex shipbuilding project management success, and defined the long-term interactions among all shipbuilding evolutions. This application became the first Systems Dynamics application to be a winner in the prestigious Edelman Global Award competition.

I incorporated what I learned from the mistakes Litton and the Navy made in the 1970s into the principles I would live by as I made the many decisions I came to face as CEO of Metro Machine during the next 34 years.

- Personally follow (yourself) all the rules you make for others.
- Always make your own phone calls and answer your own phone.
- Always be truthful to your customer, your employees and yourself.
- Always put the interest of the company ahead of your own interests.
- Always know, in detail, exactly where every project actually stands.
- Always make sure the customer is fully and honestly informed.
- Eliminate all possible obstacles to acquiring information.
- Never proceed until all prerequisites are complete.
- Never delay a decision beyond when it must be made.
- Never delay a necessary decision because you are afraid of making it.
- Never delay a necessary decision because it is inconvenient to make.
- Consider all available information when making a decision.
- Always play the hand you are holding.
- Never choose to play a hand you wish you were holding.
- Self-respect never has a price.
- Respect is an essential element of cooperation.
- No one ever respects someone who does not show them respect.
- Luck is always the main difference between you and anyone else.
- The only thing to fear is not honestly doing your best.
- When all else fails, try making your listeners laugh.
- If you succeed, they will be eager to hear what you wish to say.

Adherence to these principles and an enhanced ability to look into the future learned from using Systems Dynamics enabled Metro Machine to compete in a manner that uniquely benefited the U.S Navy, Metro Machine's employee-owners, Metro Machine's Community and the Environment.

Meanwhile, Ken Cooper successfully employed the expanded Systems Dynamics capabilities developed for the Litton Project to improve management of other comparable complex projects.

In early 2011, General Dynamics, the largest shipyard employer in the world, expressed interest in purchasing the Metro Machine stock owned by the Metro Machine ESOP. On November 1, 2011, the Metro Machine Board of Directors, after due consideration, accepted the final General Dynamics offer. Each employee's appropriate share of that amount, as audited by the IRS, has been distributed.

The total average individual 25-year compensation of Metro Machine employees, including wages, vacation, medical, dental and ESOP was, almost certainly, higher than that for any other U.S. shipyard.

Meanwhile, Metro Machine's founder turned his original 1963 investment of $10,000 into more than $20 million in 1986, showing that a company can provide good lives for its workers and still fairly reward its investors.

The skills I learned from my three Electric Boat shipyard mentors, combined with the respect for others I received from my parents and teachers, the inspiration and courage I received from Janet, the unique management skills I received from Ken Cooper, and the trust I received from Henry Swanner, enabled me to bring benefit to all who teamed with me after 1975. I looked forward to and thoroughly enjoyed every day.

The goal I pursued every day was to be the most successful shipwright of my time, while always conducting myself in an ethical manner to be a positive example for all other shipwrights.

After 34 years as a shipyard CEO, I am satisfied with:

- My annual returns to shareholders;
- The equality of employment opportunities Metro created;
- The environmental advances Metro implemented;

- The facility expansions Metro accomplished;
- The independent research and development Metro accomplished;
- The workplace safety Metro maintained;
- •The management systems Metro conceived and implemented;
- The Navy performance fees Metro earned;
- My many patented inventions;
- My civic participation and awards;
- My industry participation and awards and my academic awards; and
- That I have done all I could to achieve the goal I pursued.

Building Shipwright Success on Life's Miracles includes many of the important words and deeds of those who accompanied me on my shipyard odyssey. I was inspired to do better by those words and deeds.

After reading this book, I think you will agree with me that something unusual occurred at Metro Machine that produced the accomplishments, luck and miracles that happened there.

Part I: Shipyard Tales

Norfolk, VA. shipyard **Heinrich J. Jarczyk (1988)**

I commissioned Heinrich Jarczyk to create this etching of Metro Machine when Janet, he and I were participating in a NATO event. The etching commemorated the 25th anniversary of Metro Machine. 120 prints of the etching were made and presented individually in my office, in seniority and print order, to the 120 most senior Metro Machine employees. I was presented Number 17.

Dr. Jarczyk received a doctorate in Natural Science from Munich University. He retired from Research and Industry in 1986. His artwork is held in high regard around the world. He is my friend.

1: *Tales of the Electric Boat Shipyard (1958-1968)*

On July 13, 1958, one day after graduating from Webb Institute, I drove up the Connecticut Turnpike to Groton to start work at the Electric Boat Division of General Dynamics (Electric Boat). Electric Boat had built many of the World War II (WW II) U.S. submarines, all propelled by electric motors powered by batteries charged by diesel generators, hence the company's name. The month in 1955 when I entered Webb, Electric Boat began delivering turbine driven submarines powered by nuclear energy to the U.S. Navy. The first was Nautilus, which became a household name.

At Electric Boat, I joined the largest, most skilled collection of engineers ever assembled in a single shipyard. They had been recruited to meet the most urgent need the U.S. had after WW II.

The rocket launch of Sputnik had just demonstrated that the German scientists captured by the Russians at the end of WW II had provided the Russians with a rocket capability to deliver nuclear warheads to the U. S. As details about the Rosenberg trial became known, the World also knew the Soviets had nuclear weapons like those the U.S. had used to compel the Japanese surrender that ended World War II.

This information gave the Russians a combined capability to reach mainland U. S. with nuclear armed missiles at a time when the U.S. did not have a comparable capability to attack Russia. Presumably, there was only one thing preventing the Soviets from launching a nuclear missile attack on U.S. mainland targets in the late 1950s. It was the unavailability to the Russians of guidance and reentry technology required to target their nuclear-tipped missiles.

President Eisenhower gave his Navy just 36 months to produce a weapon system capable of retaliating against Russian intercontinental nuclear missile attacks on the U. S. before the Russians could develop their needed guidance technology. This system, contracted for joint development by Electric Boat and Lockheed, was named Polaris. Polaris was conceived to launch missiles from U. S. nuclear submarines submerged to a depth unreachable by the Russians and deployed in the

Atlantic and Arctic Oceans within range of Moscow.

The Navy established parameters for the size and number of missiles each Polaris submarine would carry. Lockheed designed and built missiles to those parameters.

Designing and building a deep submergence depth Polaris submarine was projected to take significantly more than 36 months. Therefore, it was decided that Electric Boat would initially build two nuclear submarines to Polaris parameters, excluding deep submergence depth. These were SSBN George Washington and SSBN Patrick Henry. After that, Newport News Shipbuilding, Mare Island Naval Shipyard and Portsmouth, NH Naval Shipyards would each build one shallow submergence draft submarine. As soon as the design for a deep submergence Polaris submarine was available, the same four shipyards would combine to build an additional thirty-six deep-submergence Polaris submarines.

Within 10 years of Sputnik, the U.S. would have 41 Polaris Submarines, each with two crews, containing 656 missiles targeted at Russia, to discourage Russian attack on the U.S. mainland. There has been no defense program since that was as successful.

The first important Polaris milestone event took place the week I arrived in Groton, CT in August 1958. It would be accomplished by the Electric Boat Shipwright Department where I was assigned to work. The Shipwrights slid a 1500-ton submarine section 150 feet down the ways that week, something that had never been done before! Little did I know I would be the one directing such moves in just five years.

The torpedo firing submarine SSN Scorpion was ready to launch down the ways in Groton. The Navy and Electric Boat decided it was possible to cut Scorpion in half and slide the outboard half down the ways the length of a Polaris submarine missile compartment.

Building a missile compartment in the "gap" to convert Scorpion to SSBN George Washington shaved four critical months off the time required to build George Washington from scratch. Because of this, George Washington fired its first unarmed missile on target just 36 months after Sputnik went into orbit.

The Polaris program had the highest peacetime priority ever. It was also the highest priority since that of the Manhattan project of the early 1940s. This national urgency is what attracted so many of the nation's finest engineers and physicists to Groton, CT in 1958. I was one of the third of the Webb class of 1958 who came with that group.

Tom Dunn, Webb Institute class of 1929, was the Chief Nuclear Project Engineer at Electric Boat in 1958. Tom had convinced the senior management of Electric Boat to create a one year on-the-job nuclear power plant training program for a small number of elite engineering recruits, primarily new Webb graduates.

This program gave its engineers practical work assignments in each engineering specialty; including structure, primary and secondary piping systems, mechanical and electrical systems, a nuclear project, production engineering and planning. It also provided short exposure assignments to each production department and the material control department.

Tom Dunn's program uniquely prepared its participants for shipyard work by requiring an integrated understanding of all functions performed during design and construction of complex prototype warships. After I completed the program in 1959, I used that extraordinary knowledge every day during my remaining 52 years in shipbuilding.

As that program was ending for me, I heard about a brilliant 1952 Webb valedictorian and Harvard Business School graduate named Al Zeien. He was in charge of a new and creative Electric Boat engineering department named Cost Engineering. Al Zeien was one of the famed and amazing "Whiz Kids" I had listened to and looked up to on New York Radio in the 1940s.

The Cost Engineering Department was, for the first time, applying engineering principles to the business and financial demands of designing, planning and building complex Navy ships. It was responsible for all cost estimating, budgeting, progressing and negotiating. Al Zeien convinced me during my interview that the science of meeting budgetary demands of designing, building and maintaining complex Navy ships would, someday, be just as important as meeting technical requirements.

The day Al Zeien predicted came before the end of the Polaris program, much sooner than anyone expected. Cost performance has since been the single most important responsibility of every shipyard

CEO. During my time in shipyards, no other shipyard CEO had so many years of CEO longevity as I did at Metro Machine. My three years with Al Zeien and his small band of cost engineers deserve much of the credit for that longevity. Al Zeien is now retired from Gillette where he attained the position of Chairman and CEO.

In a letter to Al written through his wife, Joyce, because of Al's Alzheimer's, I said the following:

"I just finished reading about Webb's honoring of Al in the Winter 2013-2014 Webb News. After reading that, it occurred to me that I have never discussed with Al the indispensable role he played in my career and, therefore my life. I do not think there is another Webb observer with insights into Al's shipyard career that compare to mine. Because of that, I thought you and he would be interested in my reflections of our shared shipbuilding experiences. You should know that I have thought back on our relationship thousands of times and admiringly discussed Al with others hundreds of times during the years since I last worked for him in 1968.

Unquestionably, that relationship was an integral part of my career and life and an important reason for the ultimate success of that career and fulfillment of that life. Furthermore, Al's intellectual enthusiasm was an indispensable part of the zest I felt for my work on a daily basis."

During the three years, I worked in Cost Engineering, I frequently came in contact with Norman McIntyre, Electric Boat's legendary Works Manager from WWII until the late 1960s. Mr. McIntyre knew, better than anyone, how to build submarines. He was the finest leader of men I ever encountered.

Everyone who set foot in Electric Boat had heard his name. Everyone who knew him loved and respected him. He was very approachable but stern. His demeanor made all his subordinates, peers and superiors want to earn his respect. They worked harder, smarter and more cooperatively just to please him. He had an uncanny ability to identify individuals he could trust and individuals he could not. His mere presence would calm any situation. He was always straight. He always got right to the point. He always knew what was important and what was not. You never had to wonder what he was really thinking. But when a situation triggered his anger, you did not want to be in his sight because he could see into your soul. I stood in awe of him and still do even though it has been 30 years since his passing.

Mr. McIntyre's example of how to lead is the one I tried to follow for 50 years. The importance of everything else I learned at work during my lifetime is insignificant compared to the importance of what I learned from Mr. McIntyre.

In 1963, Mr. McIntyre told Al Zeien that he wanted me to replace the Electric Boat Shipwright Superintendent, who had died suddenly. No one said no to a Norman McIntyre request, nor would Al Zeien or I ever have considered doing so.

This was the first-time Mr. McIntyre had experimented by transferring one of Electric Boat's engineers into senior production management. This job would make me the first production superintendent younger than 35 years of age in the history of Electric Boat. It threw me into a world where I would be responsible for the cost, schedule, quality and safety accomplishments of 1000 others. It threw me into a world where some over-zealous individuals tried to make themselves look good by making me look bad. It threw me, for the first time, into a world inhabited by organized labor. Up until then, I had been responsible only for my own actions.

I was 27 at the time and I jumped at the opportunity. I thrived on the experience for two years. During those two years, the Electric Boat Shipwright Department launched four Polaris submarines. The Shipwrights also drydocked George Washington and Patrick Henry for installation of advanced missile tubes. Electric Boat then acquired Bethlehem Steel's Quincy Shipyard and assigned Al Zeien the responsibility of operating it. Al Zeien and Norman McIntyre chose me for the position of Quincy General Installation Superintendent in charge of shipwrights, painters, cleaners, machinists, pipefitters, electricians and test engineers. These departments included almost half of the employees in the shipyard.

Before I left Groton for Quincy, the Shipwrights honored me by inviting me to pull the launching trigger for SSBN George Bancroft on March 20, 1965. Fifty-two years later, I can still feel the awesome power I released that day.

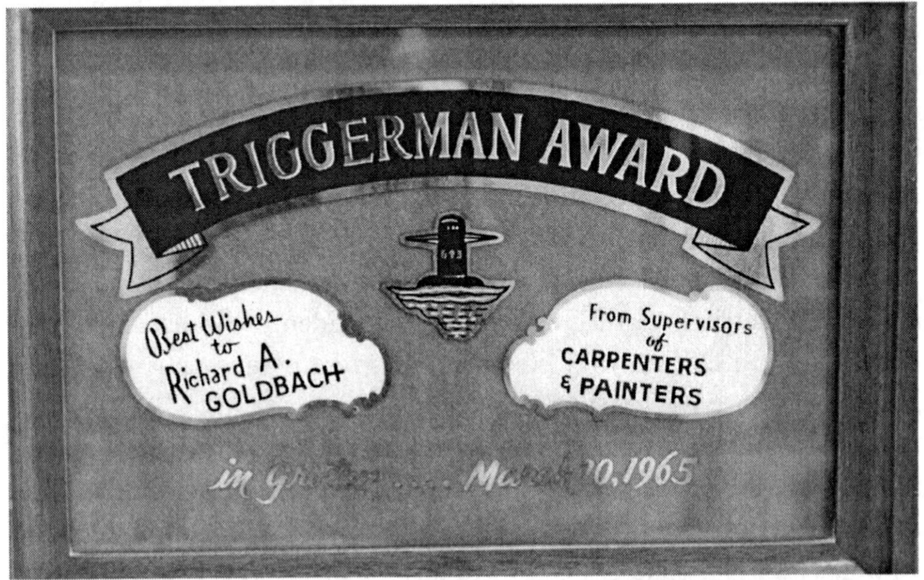

Award for pulling the launching trigger on SSBN 643 George Bancroft

I wish I could say that Al Zeien and I were the successes in Quincy we had been in Groton. We were not. Without realizing it and with the best of intentions, we had let our job responsibilities get ahead of our job capabilities. We made the mistake of thinking the fact that we had been chosen for our jobs meant we were capable of performing our jobs. Unfortunately, that was not so!

There were, of course, numerous other individuals who were responsible for the general failure present at Quincy, three years after Electric Boat acquired it. But that did not excuse the amount of time it took me to realize that my own organizations were not accomplishing their responsibilities. While I could not undo much of the damage that had been done, I promised myself that I would learn everything possible from my participation in the Quincy failure. I promised myself that I would never forget what I learned, and I never did!

Since I was only 32 at the time, this turned out to be another 43 years. Al Zeien and I both elected to leave Quincy at about the same time. Al Zeien went to Gillette and I went to a Mississippi shipyard named Ingalls, headed by a 1938 MIT naval architecture graduate named Lloyd Bergeson.

Lloyd Bergeson was an industrial engineering genius who started his career in a legendary shipyard named Cramps Shipyard in Philadelphia. He had been in charge of production control for Cramps throughout World War II, when 18,000 Cramps workers built submarines and cruisers. When Carlton Shugg, AEC Deputy General Manager, was selected to build the Nautilus as General Manager of Electric Boat, he selected Lloyd Bergeson for the position of Manager of Manufacturing Services.

In that position, Lloyd was responsible for all Electric Boat logistic support including planning, scheduling, estimating, procurement, production control and material control. Lloyd Bergeson's tireless and ingenious work is considered equally responsible, along with the work of Carlton Shugg, Tom Dunn, and Norman McIntyre, for the extraordinary schedule success of the Nautilus and Polaris programs. He had the reputation for being the most driven senior manager in shipbuilding.

Lloyd Bergeson was just the man the nation needed to drive the Nautilus and Polaris programs to meet their schedules. Credit for the all-important production timeliness of those critical programs also belongs to the management systems Lloyd Bergeson created and employed during the 1950s. Woe to anyone who stood in the way of making a schedule milestone established by Lloyd Bergeson.

Sixty years have passed since Lloyd Bergeson implemented Electric Boat's nuclear submarine management systems. Today, all medium and large U.S. shipyards are still using management systems based on Lloyd Bergeson's management systems

Lloyd had left Electric Boat at the end of the Polaris program to become general manager of the Ingalls East Bank Shipyard. While we never discussed his reasons for leaving the Electric Boat shipyard he had been instrumental in building, his leaving coincided with Carlton Shugg retiring as general manager and someone else being selected to replace him.

2: Tales of Ingalls Shipyard (1968 to 1975)

There were five unexplainable, but actual happenings that had enormous consequences for me and for others my life affected. The sequence of events leading up to the first of these was already underway in June 1968 when I reported for work to Lloyd Bergeson in Pascagoula, Mississippi.

The U.S. Navy had just awarded Ingalls a contract to construct three torpedo firing nuclear attack submarines. These submarines were similar to five torpedo-firing nuclear attack submarines EB had constructed, along with Polaris submarines, during the ten years, I was employed there.

The Navy had also encouraged Ingalls to become capable of overhauling and refueling nuclear submarines. The job Lloyd Bergeson hired me for was Director of Submarine Overhaul reporting to him. I was responsible for building a new drydock and a new Radiation Control (RADCON) facility to control the required nuclear work. I was also responsible for all nuclear submarine overhaul planning.

Lloyd Bergeson subsequently assigned me the additional position of Director of Planning for the East Bank Shipyard. In addition to Submarine Overhaul, this position included manpower planning, scheduling, production control, material control, estimating, industrial engineering and facilities; all-in-all a lot of responsibility for a 32-year-old shipwright. I felt honored that Lloyd would consider me for this position, which was essentially the same one Lloyd had held at Electric Boat.

The Navy experienced a six-month procurement delay in awarding the submarine contract to Ingalls. In an attempt to prevent this contract award delay from delaying submarine deliveries, the Navy purchased all the steel needed for the three submarines itself instead of having Ingalls buy it in accordance with the contract.

The Navy procurement system, while capable of buying big things like ships, is not set up to buy small things like pieces of steel.

Therefore, the Navy was unable to acquire the steel in a manner that was timely or organized. As a result, when the submarine steel that was needed at the start of submarine construction finally arrived, it arrived too late to employ the steel workers who had been assembled to fabricate it during the scheduled window. Compounding the problem, the delayed submarine steel required Ingalls to accomplish nuclear submarine steel fabrication during a scheduled window already reserved for Ingalls' non-submarine steel fabrication.

Then, the Navy issued a change to the submarine contract establishing the actual steel delivery dates as the revised contract dates.

The Ingalls estimating department, which was responsible for determining cost and schedule impacts of such occurrences, estimated the cost of Ingalls delay and disruption caused by late steel delivery. It then properly certified the estimate and made a proper claim for the alleged added cost. The Navy disputed the amount claimed. After negotiations failed to resolve the differences, the matter was referred to DOD's Armed Service Board of Contract Appeals (ASBCA), which routinely heard the matter and ruled in Ingalls' favor. I was one of Ingalls' rebuttal witnesses in the 1973 ASBCA hearing.

After the ASBCA hearing, I was advised that Admiral Hyman Rickover, the Patriarch of the Naval Reactors Program, reportedly resented the added procurement costs for "his" nuclear ships and had alleged to the Department of Justice that there had to have been fraud in the Ingalls claim. Despite the legal finding of the Government's own ASBCA civil court to the contrary, Admiral Rickover demanded a Federal criminal grand jury be empaneled to investigate the Ingalls claim.

This demand ultimately resulted in four separate grand juries investigating the Ingalls claim over four years. One of these was by a special grand jury that was purported to be the longest special grand jury ever held. I was to come to know this special grand jury well.

Because the Ingalls estimating department that prepared the claim reported to me, I was named a "Target of the Investigation". My case was separated from the Ingalls case. I was assigned separate lawyers, independent of those representing Ingalls. They were Bingo and Freddie Stant, who had previously represented executives of several Norfolk, Virginia shipyards in fraud investigations.

As disconcerting as the Rickover investigation was, I was about to find out my real problems were just starting:

The demands of Grand Jury and FBI testifying were quite distracting for me during a time when corporate infighting was starting to take place in Litton because of the horrendous performance of the new Ingalls West Bank Shipyard. The Ingalls West Bank Shipyard, which was significantly behind schedule on the Navy's two largest shipbuilding programs, had become the laughing stock of the shipyard industry and a political liability for the venerable Senator John Stennis of Mississippi and Navy Secretary John Warner.

The Ingalls East Bank shipyard, where I was working, was performing well on its Navy obligations, including those of Admiral Rickover's three nuclear submarines. Nonetheless, the Navy advised Litton that it would accept no more bids from either the Ingalls East Bank shipyard or West Bank shipyard until Litton solved the Ingalls West Bank Shipyard problems.

In 1974, I was assigned to head a high-priority Litton task force established for the purpose of organizationally combining the Ingalls East Bank Shipyard with the Ingalls West Bank Shipyard. Members of the task force were confined to the Longfellow House in Pascagoula day and night for a week. At the end of this week, we presented our comprehensive recommendations to the most senior Litton management, including Chairman Harry Grey.

After this presentation, I was additionally assigned the same West Bank Shipyard functions I was already performing for the East Bank Shipyard.

When I started to get involved with the West Bank shipyard, I found out that Litton had been asserting that the underlying cause of its West Bank shipbuilding problem was that the Navy made damaging decisions and design changes it had no contractual authority to make. Meanwhile the Navy believed and was asserting that the underlying cause of Ingalls' West Bank shipbuilding problems was Litton's failure to adequately contend with Shipyard-of-the-Future startup problems. I very quickly became convinced that there was plenty of responsibility for the obvious West Bank shipbuilding problems to go around.

Since neither side was in a position to make concessions, this significant difference had resulted in a "Mexican Standoff". Litton could not concede to the Navy without admitting to Wall Street that its rosy projections of "Shipyard of the Future" shipbuilding profits were overstated and its stock price was too high. The Navy could not concede to Litton without admitting to Congress and the public that it was unable to manage shipbuilding budget overruns, risking future budget cuts from Congress.

In my new position, I became the primary spokesperson for Ingalls when the many high level Directors, Navy officials, bankers, investors and politicians visited to hear what Ingalls was doing to fix its West Bank shipbuilding programs. Nothing in my life had prepared me for such a role.

In the early 1960s, encouraged by the Kennedy Administration, DOD had the Navy implement a significantly different ship procurement approach called Total Package Procurement (TPP). Robert McNamara, Secretary of Defense, based the decision on the fact that the Air Force had used TPP effectively when procuring large numbers of airplanes.

The Air Force administered its TPP contracts using a much more hands-off approach by allowing its contractors to meet specified performance criteria. The Navy had never used this approach. Instead, the Navy solicited shipbuilding bids using contract plans and specifications that constrained the design latitude of its shipbuilders. Litton asserted that by the Navy using a TPP contract approach on its Litton ships, it had given Litton the same design flexibility for its ships that the Air Force gives TPP contract aircraft manufacturers for its planes.

Whatever the facts were regarding the Navy's contractual intent, the Navy managed the Litton ship designs much as it had before TPP. When Litton was awarded two TPP contracts worth over $3 billion, it proceeded to construct an all-new Litton Shipyard of the Future costing $130 million.

Consistent with its understanding of TPP, Litton asserted it planned ship designs in a manner that assumed there would be little or no Government participation in the design process for its two awarded TPP contracts. This included elimination of most Government approvals of most working drawings.

Litton claimed that as the Kennedy and Johnson administrations left office, the Navy returned to the same approach to control the TPP design of the Litton ships it had used before TPP. Litton claimed further that this resumption had eliminated any possibility for Litton employing the streamlined design process that Litton's bids had anticipated.

Meanwhile, Litton was awarded an eight-ship container ship construction contract it intended to use to debug its new Shipyard of the Future before using that shipyard to build its TPP Navy ships. These commercial container ships obviously could not have had any of the design problems Litton alleged had taken place on its TPP Navy Contracts. Yet, Litton ship construction performance on these non-Navy container ships was appalling and of great concern to the Navy.

Any knowledgeable person fairly examining the two issues would have to agree that both the Navy and Litton had significant responsibility for the overwhelming problems that were experienced on the two TPP contracts. But the political arena of the day on these two largest Navy contracts of all time, was not conducive to a fair examination of the facts and allocation of responsibility.

Search for the facts of the matter was more complicated by the fact that Litton started its ship design in Los Angeles, but then moved it to Pascagoula with significant disruption of design personnel.

The Navy had traditionally procured most of its destroyers from an historic shipyard named Bath Iron Works, the largest employer in Maine, which had a very fine reputation with Navy personnel. Maine's most influential politician of the day was the legendary Margaret Chase Smith, Chair of the Senate Republican Conference.

Republicans were in the minority in the Senate and a Democrat held the White House (Kennedy/Johnson). Bath and Senator Margaret Chase Smith had strongly opposed TPP for the destroyer procurement from the beginning because it made it most difficult, if not impossible, for Bath to participate in the procurement

The most influential senator of the time was Democratic Senator John Stennis of Mississippi, Chairman of the U.S. Committee on Armed Forces and one of the most powerful and respected men in Washington. He naturally endorsed TPP because it had provided a decade of work to his state's largest employer.

Navy personnel, in part because TPP was an Air Force airplane procurement practice which they considered inappropriate for procuring ships and partly because of the confidence they had in Bath, were unenthusiastic about TPP. Some were also unenthusiastic about the successful bidder TPP gave them for building their much-needed destroyers.

Since the working drawings needed for ship construction were not available in time to acquire material for and accomplish the millions of specific production tasks required to construct each ship, each production task was performed inefficiently and with a lot of rework. This created an additional need for more and more production workers to cope with the confusion and somehow get it right. The Ingalls need for additional workers drained the Gulf Coast of skilled workers, causing an increased use of semi-skilled workers, who were less efficient than the skilled workers planned.

It is common shipbuilding industry knowledge that the operating efficiency of every shipyard is most dependent on work being performed in the optimum sequence. This optimum sequence was unattainable at Litton under the circumstances. Performing work out of sequence therefore had yet another negative effect on schedule performance and efficiency of West Bank shipwrights.

But I saw an even bigger problem that was unique to Litton's financial management plan approach plus the inability or unwillingness of the Navy and Litton to officially agree to share responsibility for cost and schedule overruns. This problem was having a catastrophic, but hidden, effect on both ship cost and schedule.

Every six months, in response to recognized cost overruns on the earlier already-accomplished work, budget and schedule edicts were issued by the President of Ingalls. By these edicts, he directed accountants and manpower planners to deduct budgeted overruns on completed work from the budgets for un-started work. This minimized the reported contract cost overruns for the time being. But, since the Litton management approach also demanded manning plans be consistent with financial budgets, the planned manning for un-started work was significantly understated. This caused later and later accomplishment of work that was prerequisite to all other work and a cascade of cost and schedule impacts of enormous magnitude.

Frustration and unjustified blaming resulting from this was causing resignations, firings and organizational instability among normally competent middle-level production managers. This compounded all the other problems.

The overall problem was going to be significant under any circumstances. But, I concluded it could be reduced somewhat with the acquiescence of the Litton Corporate Controller. The approach I concluded was necessary would allow Ingalls' operating plans for manning to match actual needs, even if those needs were inconsistent with Corporate financial plans.

I suspected that some or all of the Litton Board Members had some level of unrevealed suspicion that things were much worse than they were being presented by management. But, I was certain that none of them were aware of how much worse the situation was becoming because of Ingalls not being able to schedule its planned manning around the problems that had already occurred.

My proposed change had important implications because it would expose significant projected program delays and cost increases of which the Board of Directors had no official knowledge. Therefore, I believed Ingalls needed to advise Board of Directors members and get some level of consensus from them before it actually took the action.

Ingalls had its semi-annual financial plan presentation to the Board of Directors coming in a couple of weeks. As usual, I was to be one of the primary presenters. I called a meeting of all my companion executives reporting to the President and convinced them to join me in presenting this problem to the Board of Directors after first discussing that presentation with the President.

It was agreed by all members of the President's staff that my proposed action had to be taken and that the best time to discuss the proposal with the President would be during one of the rehearsals we normally held with him. These rehearsed presentations were held in his office in order to give him an opportunity to both comment on and approve what we would say.

Unfortunately, while everyone on his staff heard what I planned to say numerous times and endorsed it, the President never did. Whenever my turn to address him came, he said he had to use the bathroom and to proceed without him.

I now believe the President intentionally avoided hearing what I planned to say so he could later deny knowledge of and responsibility for the problem he had caused by his edicts. At the time, I believed the President's failure to listen to what I planned to say was unfortunate, but that Ingalls still had an obligation to stockholders to reduce the huge and growing problem it had.

As a result, the first time the President heard my presentation was when I made it to the full Board of Directors, including its Chairman. I was immensely relieved after making my presentation and bringing the huge problem to the attention of the Board of Directors. At last, Ingalls could start resolving one of the biggest problems it had.

As I left the room, I was pleased that most of my fellow Staff members grabbed for my hand. A few said, "Thanks – Great Job." I went back to my office, sat at my desk and savored the moment, which I very briefly considered to be my most important management moment ever.

In just minutes, the President came charging into my office, actually frothing at the mouth, with Harry Grey, the Litton Chairman of the Board following him.

You F______G B______D. You will pay for not telling me you were going to do this!

I tried to remind the President that he had always left the room whenever I was about to advise him what everyone working for him had heard and agreed that the Board needed to be told. The President just continued saying horrible and disgusting things clearly intended to humiliate me in front of Chairman Harry Grey, a man I respected and believed also respected me. Then, the President left as abruptly as he had arrived, with Harry Grey following.

I was washed up and possibly facing prison with no future at Ingalls. I was 39 with five dependents including Janet's parents.

I received the call several days later. I was told I would not be discharged because of the Company's dependence on my Grand Jury and FBI testimony during Admiral Rickover's Submarine still-continuing witch hunt. Instead, I was assigned to Litton's Project X, which had been created to prepare Litton's claim against the Navy on the West Bank Shipyard's Destroyer and Amphibious Ship Programs, the largest shipyard claim ever made against the Navy - Just what I needed as a Target of the Submarine Claim FBI Investigation.

I would be interrogated monthly on the submarine claim by the Special Grand Jury and regularly by teams of up to 20 FBI agents taking turns grilling me. For the first year of the submarine investigation, I was terrified and ashamed that my innocent family might somehow be unfairly hurt by things I was falsely being accused of doing. I made the terrible mistake of cowardly withdrawing from my family and avoiding talking about the investigation with Dad, Janet and everyone else. I now know how afraid this made Janet feel.

One weekend, when my parents were visiting from Maryland, I had to drive from Mobile to Pascagoula and back to pick up a document, a round trip of about two hours. Dad asked if I wanted company. I said "sure". After forty years, I can still picture the exact place on the Grand Bay, Alabama back road I was driving on when the first incredibly difficult words came out. Then they came faster. Then, they became a waterfall. They continued on the trip back after I completed whatever I had to do in Pascagoula that day. Sometime before we arrived home, I was done.

Dad, the World's greatest listener, had listened to every one of my words without speaking. When I stopped, Dad simply asked: "Did you ever do anything wrong?" I replied, "No". He said, "Then you don't really have anything to worry about, do you?" I said, "I guess not".

How could I have missed for all that time that it was only whether I did anything wrong that mattered? And, I hadn't done anything wrong! I had created my nightmare all by myself, entirely in my own mind. And now it was over!

I realized that I had dealt with my setbacks and fears poorly and treated Janet terribly. I knew I had to tell Janet all I had told Dad, including my fear of being put in jail, and I did. When I finished, Janet said, "If you ever have to go away, I will be waiting for you when you come back."

I have lived almost 43 years since Janet said that. In some of those early years, I had to face up to harsh, intimidating and unrelenting interrogation. Later years required me to take very significant long-term personal and family financial risks to induce banks to meet the financial needs of Metro Machine and its employee-owners.

But, after Janet's simple statement that day, no matter what I faced, I never again felt fear. I woke up every day knowing nothing could keep me from doing my best for everyone who had put their trust in me, whatever my best and their needs happened to be that day.

I know I would have achieved none of the success I did without the courage Janet gave me for life that day.

There were originally just two FBI agents sent to Ingalls to interview Ingalls' employees. One of the two lead FBI agents assigned to the Ingalls matter was agent Ross Graben. Ross Graben was one of the finest men I ever encountered and a credit to the service. I was pleased to have the opportunity to tell him so many years later after he retired from the service and he called me for advice on a non-FBI matter.

There was a second lead agent who used an intimidating approach full of bluster, insults, ignorance and innuendo. Perhaps he was the "bad cop" end of a "good cop/bad cop" routine, but he didn't seem to be acting. One time, the FBI flooded Ingalls with more than 20 agents asking questions of many Ingalls employees, none of whom professed any knowledge of Ingalls wrong-doing.

I became the most frequent witness testifying before the special grand jury investigating Ingalls. I was represented by the attorney retained to represent me named Bingo Stant of Norfolk, Virginia. Inevitably, we got to discussing shipyards. Bingo often talked to me about another shipyard client he had named Henry Swanner. He told me Henry was looking for someone to manage a shipyard business he had bought for $10,000 that was now worth over a million dollars. He told me he thought Henry and I would like each other because we each had what the other needed and we would trust each other. He told Henry the same thing.

Henry and I started talking every time I came up to Virginia to testify to the special grand jury in the Alexandria, Virginia Federal Court House. It turned out that Henry had Federal investigation issues not unlike mine. We came to agree that, if we could both be successful in our investigation experiences, we would become partners. Meanwhile, Bingo Stant was working with both of us to do his part to make sure that day would come.

One day in 1976, the other lead FBI agent, a large man, came over to my Project X office to tell me an incredible story about Litton Chairman Harry Grey conspiring with criminal elements to do great harm to the United States. He told me he had incriminating evidence which would prove his statement, but that he could only show me the evidence off Ingalls property.

I didn't really believe him, but felt I could not ignore him either. Whatever I thought of him, he was a law enforcement officer of the United States Government. I agreed to follow him in my car. He drove to a remote cabin. The cabin was in a location unfamiliar to me which was deep in a Mississippi forest.

After we entered the one-room cabin that was his destination, he pulled out a bottle of Wild Turkey bourbon, which he apparently knew to be my drink, and poured a hefty glass for both himself and me and then put both glasses on the table between us.

He gulped his. I sipped mine. Then he proceeded to demand answers to the same questions I had been answering for over a year during the investigation. I repeatedly demanded he show me the incriminating evidence he had told me he had and had brought me out to see. He repeatedly ignored my request and continued to grill me by asking the same questions different ways. As he did, he continued to gulp his Wild Turkey as I continued to sip mine. He became increasingly incoherent and threatened to start digging up my yard and digging into my sex life. I told him to help himself. Since his unjustified investigation had already destroyed my sex life, I had nothing to lose.

When I couldn't take his rantings any more, I simply got up and walked out. I somehow found my way out of the forest. He did not hinder me in any way.

It was reported to me that this same agent got drunk regularly at the Longfellow House Bar down the street from the Ingalls East Bank Shipyard. I was told that, when he did, he told anyone who would listen what crooks the managers of Ingalls were. I heard later that, perhaps because his performance at Ingalls was considered unsatisfactory, the FBI had transferred him to a remote FBI office out in the desert somewhere. I don't recall ever seeing him after that night in the forest.

The special grand jury empaneled to hear evidence pertaining to the Ingalls submarine investigation in 1975 was reported to be the longest special federal grand jury ever enacted by the Justice Department. It was the third grand jury to hear evidence on the Ingalls investigation since the first two failed to return any indictments.

Each time the Ingalls' special Grand Jury met to take evidence and hear testimony, I would be subpoenaed to give testimony. The U.S. Attorney, who led the Grand Jury questioning, asked many of the same questions each time and always got the same answers from me since they were based on facts I had in my records.

My last Grand Jury testimony was in Alexandria in March 1977, when the special grand jury was scheduled to end its investigation. The statute of limitations pertaining to me would expire at midnight. The U.S. Attorney asked if I would volunteer to meet with him briefly, without the Grand Jury members and my lawyers being present. After consulting with Bingo, I agreed.

That supposedly brief meeting took place in a private chamber. It involved the same old questions asked over and over again by numerous Government lawyers and over 10 FBI agents. I finally called it quits after over six hours. I told them to do whatever they had to do and I would do whatever I had to do. As I walked out, I said, "I'm going to look a whole lot better after the trial than you are!".

Freddie Stant, Bingo's son, met me outside the chamber to tell me he had just been advised by the Government that it would let the statute of limitations expire on me without making an indictment. He also told me Henry Swanner and I could now proceed with our agreement to partner. I called Janet as soon as I could to tell her the important news.

I planned to spend the night sleeping in the cellar of my parents' Rockville, Maryland home. When Rob and I went off to Webb Institute, my Mom had set up our twin beds there; mattresses, box springs and all. Sleeping in the same bed for which I had left my crib seemed to be especially comforting that night.

It was to turn out that this night was to be as pivotal for my next forty years as that move from the crib had been for my first forty years.

My Mom and Dad were out playing bridge when I arrived at their house. I remember assuming my Mom was crowing loudly as usual when she finessed the PHDs of Applied Physics Laboratory.

I sat down at Dad's desk to write him the longest letter I had ever written to him. It was his and Janet's strength and integrity that had gotten me through the last three years. I didn't mind that my letter was wet when I put it under his pillow and assume he didn't mind it was wet when he read it.

The Justice Department empaneled a new one-day special grand jury that returned an indictment against Litton for Criminal Fraud. This fourth grand jury heard evidence only from two FBI agents, making sure no facts could stand in the way of satisfying Admiral Rickover. The Federal Court in Alexandria, Virginia heard the Government's case and dismissed it for prosecutorial misconduct. The Government appealed the decision and won a retrial. Litton demanded and was given a Change of Venue to Mississippi. The Mississippi Federal Court trial found for Litton.

More than five years had passed since Admiral Rickover had made his original unfounded and unsubstantiated allegations that caused so much unjustified grief for so many patriotic Americans. A great American had done a very wrong thing at the end of a brilliant career. His harmful allegations had wastefully occupied a multitude of Government and Litton employees for almost six years. He was almost 80 years old and near the mandatory retirement age.

When I was banished to Project X in 1975, the project had, for years, been the dumping ground for every Ingalls employee the company felt it no longer had a purpose for but did not want to face up to firing. It employed hundreds of workers chosen only because they were not wanted anymore, with little regard to whether they were qualified to accomplish the work required. Project X was getting nowhere when I arrived there because nobody was really in charge, nobody really had a clue what the objective was and nobody had been selected based on their qualifications for their assigned functions. Like me, everyone was there because someone working someplace else didn't want them around anymore.

Hoped-for income from Project X by Litton at that time was well into the hundreds of millions of dollars and growing. Additional contract costs caused by the additional program delays being announced every six months were being financially offset by unjustified increases to forecasted revenues from Project X. Litton's independent accountants apparently concluded that no increased TPP Contract loss needed to be reported to stockholders because of Project X, even though there was yet to be one dollar of cost officially claimed from the Government.

3: *Tales of Project X (1975-1977)*

My 1975 banishment was to a Project X trailer office looking out at a field of overgrown weeds in one of Pascagoula's poorest neighborhoods. It was miles away from any shipyard work or workers. The local kids seemed to have adopted the weeds just outside my one window as a public toilet. Yelling at them and pounding on the window to startle them didn't seem to discourage them. Most of the time I just put my head down on the desk and felt sorry for myself.

To this day, I still consider that several-month period to be the very bottom of my existence.

I was assigned one empty desk with one desk chair in the trailer office. No one gave me anything to do and I didn't look for anything to do. It seemed almost no one wanted to or dared to talk to me. Uncharacteristically, I didn't even have an interest in reading. The only thing I had to look forward to each day was the "peanut man" showing up at noon selling peanuts in the shell, one of my favorites. I'd give him some quarters, take the peanuts back to my office and eat them as I tried in vain to once more chase away the kids. The peanuts were causing me to gain weight.

Some days I wished there was something I could say to the FBI that would bring the investigation to an end. But there wasn't, because the only thing that would satisfy Admiral Rickover was an Ingalls admission of wrongdoing and no Ingalls wrongdoing had ever taken place. Microscopic and repeated FBI questioning had convinced me that I had never told or asked anyone to do anything illegal or unethical. No one, including the President, had ever asked me or told me to do anything illegal or unethical. I simply had never done anything illegal or unethical. I was trapped with no apparent way out because no other employers would consider me once they learned my availability was questionable until the Grand Jury process played out.

It took a month or two of lecturing myself for me to start realizing that my family was depending on me to somehow solve this problem. No one else was going to solve it for me. The problem was mine and I had to start doing something. And certainly there was work waiting to be done in Project X, even though it was being mismanaged and no one had given me anything to do.

I became curious and made a social call on the fellow in the office next to mine. His name was John Landry. His adjustment process was four or five months ahead of mine. He was spending all his time sending out job applications. After considering whether I should do the same, I realized I was pretty much anchored to Ingalls and Project X until the FBI investigation was over.

I asked John Landry if anyone had ever given him any assignments associated with Project X. He replied that he understood he was assigned to a group that was to evaluate production impact on LHAs and destroyers, but that he had never been asked to do anything related to Project X. I asked him if he had a boss. He said he understood his boss was a man named Doc Rawlings, whose office was around the corner, but that he had rarely met with Doc. I asked John if he had ever had any association with shipyard production or any other production that qualified him to evaluate shipyard production impacts. He said, "No".

I rounded up another side chair and began inviting John into my office to chew the fat, which initially was mostly about his job hunting. He seemed to be far more nonchalant on the subject than I was. He said several times, "I have time for one more bad move and one more good move." I had no idea what he meant, but the thought seemed to satisfy him.

One day I told John that I was starting to think Ingalls problems on the Destroyer and Amphibious Programs were, in part, caused by Navy responsible design actions driving up the size of the Litton design organization. Because of its larger size, the Litton design organization performed at a lower level of efficiency and competence that rippled through downstream production support and production organizations, making them larger, less efficient and less competent.

John was always a polite and attentive listener but he rarely gave opinions of his own. Even so, just having someone to listen to my ideas started to get my mind working again. Even if John didn't have many thoughts of his own, he understood mine. Talking at John surely was more interesting than trying to scare away kids. I pulled the shade down and left it down. It never went back up. Meanwhile,

I thought more and more about the effect of organizational size on shipyard organization competency and efficiency, a subject that I knew had never previously been explored by either Electric Boat or Ingalls.

After bouncing my thoughts off John for a number of weeks, I paid a call on Archie Dunn, Director of Contracts, who was listed on the Organization Chart as the senior staff manager responsible for Project X. Archie was an acquaintance of some 15 years and one of the few Ingalls managers still willing to be seen talking with me.

In reality, Archie knew no more than I did about the substance of Project X. Neither did anyone else, even though it had been around for years. All either of us really knew about Project X was that Litton was telling its public accountants it was going to receive a huge amount of money from it.

I told Archie about my thoughts on the competency and efficiency of shipyard organizations relative to size. I always respected Archie and considered him to be well informed on the Navy ship design process. I knew he had been responsible for administration of the Electric Boat design effort for a number of years before coming to Ingalls.

I told Archie I was willing to pursue the facts of Project X for Litton, but only if it could be done in a manner that did not leave me vulnerable to future Government claim witch hunts. Archie understood my position and agreed with my conditions.

I told Archie that my approach to achieving these objectives would necessarily start with an exhaustive library search of any and all authoritative information ever published on the subject of the effect organizational size has on the competency and efficiency of large complex organizations. I told him that establishing such a foundation at the start was the only way to assure that Ingalls and I could defend ourselves in the future against Government unsubstantiated allegations, like those made on the Ingalls submarine claim. It was the only way Ingalls could readily prove in the future that it had truthfully considered all information pertinent to all aspects of the Project X claim.

I told him the search I envisioned would start with the Library of Congress in Washington, then to the National Management Association (NMA) Library in Manhattan, then to the Harvard Business School and Sloan School Libraries in Boston. I told Archie that I needed John Landry's assistance because of the magnitude of the library research planned. Archie approved my plan and so I promptly proceeded to execute it.

Because of his faith in me that day, Archie deservedly earned the credit for being the one who solved the Project X riddle. As he did, he and Ken Cooper of Pugh Roberts Associates were presented the prestigious Franz Edelman Award for creating one of the most outstanding examples of Operations Research, Management Science and Advanced Analytics in the World.

The plan initially looked very promising at the Library of Congress based on the magnitude of data which the search by Dewey Decimal System identity seemed to indicate was on the shelves. John and I were both full of enthusiasm. But, as the day wore on, each and every listing came up empty. After completely striking out at the Library of Congress on both days, we left early for Manhattan and the NMA Library. Again, we struck out in the afternoon of the first day. This great idea of mine surely didn't look so great after all. We were both disheartened. I needed a boost.

I called Janet's best high school friend, Nancy Morgan, who lived in Manhattan. She was cute and was still single. I told her I was unhappy and sure would enjoy her company. She said her evening was open so we went to the restaurant she recommended.

I was depressed about the failure of my past two days, the possibility of jail and my blown career. It made for a night of drinking and whining. I assume we ate but don't remember it. All I remember is doing a lot of talking that must have seemed endless to Nancy. She sure earned Janet's lifetime friendship that night!

This was 1975 when, although I didn't know it, I still had two years of Grand Jury Investigations ahead of me and had no idea what I would be doing to earn a salary for the rest of my life.

The result was predictable. After dinner, I dropped Nancy off at her apartment door and stumbled back into the taxi that took me to my hotel. The next morning, I skipped breakfast because I was hung over and belatedly joined John Landry at the NMA library, where he was cheerfully and methodically renewing our search.

After a good half hour of just sitting there watching John working, I started to feel guilty and stood up to give him some moral support. I was still unable to do any real work so, just for show, I started to pull books randomly off the shelves and leaf through their indexes.

Suddenly, through bleary eyes, I miraculously saw a very brief mention in the index of one of the books I had blindly pulled from a shelf of the effect of design organizational size on efficiency. Quickly turning to the referenced text, I found only two partial pages on the subject. They were part of a short discussion on something I'd never heard of called Systems Dynamics.

This turned out to be the second of the five unexplainable happenings that would significantly change my life and the lives of the many others, who would come to put their trust in me!

The author of the book, Ed Roberts, was an MIT professor who taught Systems Dynamics. I immediately called Professor Roberts who said he might meet with me later in the day, if he had time. John and I quickly left the NMA library and climbed on the shuttle to Boston. We skipped the Harvard Business School Library and headed right for the Sloan School library, where I found another copy of Professor Roberts' book but no other books on the subject. I called Professor Roberts again. He seemed quite distant. I told him that this could be very big. He agreed to meet if we could wait an hour or so.

When we met, Professor Roberts stated that he had no interest in Project X, but he had a relationship with a consulting company that might be interested in working with me on the project. The name of that company was Pugh Roberts. Within several days, Ed Roberts and Ken Cooper from Pugh Roberts were sitting with John and me in my trailer office. I again had to round up more chairs so we could all sit down at the same time. I made sure my shade was closed to keep the nosy kids out of our meeting.

Ken Cooper's letters to me describe, much better than I ever could, how he and I, working with System Dynamics, were able to get Litton and the Navy to resolve their differences and build the five LHAs and thirty destroyers the Nation badly needed. Over the years following that day, I would repair many of those ships and meet the men who commanded them. I was always proud to tell them I had helped deliver their ships to the Navy.

As Ken and I worked together, I found myself absorbing the logic of Systems Dynamics into my own logic system. This eventually provided me with my own personal Crystal Ball. I would use this Crystal Ball to frustrate all of my competitors for the next 35 years.

Letter from Ken Cooper to Janet and Me on our 50th Wedding Anniversary in July 2010

One of the happier days in my life was the day that I met Janet. I was thrilled that Rich had such an extraordinary partner in life, someone so smart and sweet and gracious. (It was only later that I learned she was also something of, well, a clown...which is to say more correctly, a world-class magician.)

The occasion of Janet & Rich's 50th wedding anniversary celebration brings this memory to mind. And it caused me to think, why would knowing Janet bring me such great joy? Why, of course, is Rich.

My friendship with Rich goes back just 35 years. Throughout that time, he has been an overwhelmingly strong and wonderful influence on me, professionally and personally.

Rich...just as you have touched and inspired and improved the lives of so many through your friendship, mentoring and love, you inspired and transformed my life through your example of principled courage, intellectual vision, and personal integrity. For you and Janet, some heartfelt memories...

...You notoriously located Ed Roberts's book by wandering the aisles of the library and looking through each index...then tracked down Ed at MIT, leading our paths to cross.

...Your original multi-color diagram of "Engineering Delay & Disruption" impacts

...Designing and building together the first simulation model ever capable of describing and quantifying those "Engineering Delay & Disruption" impacts on shipbuilding programs.

...And "Sure, we can extend this to Production, too" was a leap of faith –and audacity—I only recently came to recognize.

...Your dragging Doc Rawlings and John Landry into acceptance of the model and the analysis results, a preface to the dramatic and successful showdown with the Navy.

...Not without some little human dramas along the way...getting ready for the big claims submittal required some weekends, and when I had to be at home with my newborn son, you traveled to New Hampshire, and you, the senior Litton executive, babysat Jason – diaper changes and all – while I worked on the model analyses.

...Then leading the charge with Archie Dunn to help us win in the "Nobel Prize" of Management Science, the Edelman Award competition for the best use of management science in the world.

Many years can go between our talks, but we shared so much so intensely together, that you have been and shall always be among my closest and dearest friends.

Love & happiness always, Ken

Letter from Ken to Me on my 11/11/11 Retirement from Metro Machine

Dear Rich,

Congratulations on the honors you will get and deserve on your Metro retirement, and sincere thanks for letting me take part.

I won't even try to capture in a note all that you mean to me, but some things need to be mentioned.

...At a crucial stage in my life, after my father had just died and I had just started at Pugh-Roberts, you came along and changed everything for the better...

...Intellectually first, you defined and organized a problem never before solved, and we proceeded to solve it together.

...As a businessman, you taught and showed me how truly successful people build that success. I followed your example, and Pugh-Roberts became legendary under that leadership model (yours).

...Above all, as a person, you taught & showed me how to stand tall in the good times and the bad, that generosity and true character always prevail eventually, and that aiming high, along with the risks that it brings, is the only path to satisfying yourself that you've done all you can for your friends, family, colleagues, those in need of help, and humankind.

In short, you have shaped me to be who I am, and I am forever grateful to you, and grateful that you are my lifelong friend.

With much love and admiration

Letter from Ken to Me on June 21, 2014 – Upon My Receiving an Honorary Doctorate Degree from Webb Institute and Giving the Commencement Address

Dear Rich,

I was so happy to sit with Janet in the ceremony today—no one was beaming more that we were (ok, John too I'm sure). Your talk tugged a lot of heartstrings and brought gasps as you concluded your personal story of the importance of the American worker. It was beautiful.

As good as that was, I have to admit to enjoying at least as much our pre-lunch talk. It was great to have the "private" time, even sharing it with George and the others who followed.

I'm sorry I had to slip out without a real goodbye, but I didn't want to walk out during a later speaker.

Before I board my flight, I'm also emailing Ed to tell him about today. He will enjoy that, and appreciate the poetry of it.

I know you have Janet and Rob and John there tonight, but you also have me with you there, in my heart.

You remain my inspiration, Dr. Goldbach, my great friend, Rich.

After the Ingalls' President destroyed my Ingalls' career, he devised an apparent scheme for providing for his own future. That scheme seemed to me to be designed to enable him to be paid a substantial salary without doing any difficult work.

He declared that he was resigning as President of Ingalls to assume the position of President of the East Bank Shipyard only, which had almost no work at the time. After making that announcement, he moved into the vacant East Bank executive office suite of Ellis Gardner, the retired Ingalls Chairman who had departed Pascagoula.

Litton appointed a new Ingalls President to take his place who quickly removed the East Bank Shipyard President from his plushy East Bank office digs and fired him. Following that, the new President took destroyer and amphibious ship corrective actions consistent with those I had been fired for recommending to the Board of Directors.

His corrective actions restored reason to the Ingalls West Bank Shipbuilding Program.

I heard a rumor that the wife of the first President had divorced him and that he was living by himself in the desert with a motorcycle and monster sound system. I hoped the rumor was true, but put it into the too-good-to-be-true category. I still can't help feeling such an ending was well-deserved. But, I wish I were a strong enough person to forgive him for humiliating me!

Meanwhile, our Systems Dynamics solution to resolving the seven-year dispute between the Navy and the Ingalls West Bank Shipyard was entering its concluding stages. It turned out that this meant I had worked my way out of my only available Ingalls job.

I called on the new President to make sure Ingalls had no other plans for me. He stated that I would first have to prove myself. I told him I thought I had already done that and left.

After this discussion, Henry and I cemented our agreement to partner. We did it simply by shaking hands and looking each other in the eye. One handshake and the Metro Machine CEO position Bingo Stant had described to me three years earlier during Alexandria Grand Jury hearings was finally mine! Henry and I both realized neither of us had any hope of success if we couldn't trust each other's word.

There were a few old Ingalls friends who saw me off in the local pizzeria. I was yet to realize it, but the worst things ever to happen to me: the vindictive actions of Admiral Rickover and the Ingalls President, would turn out to be the best things ever to happen to me (except Janet, of course).

After moving to Metro Machine, I remained interested in the progress being made to energize the "Shipyard of the Future" after the president, who fired me, was removed and the management obstacles to production improvement were also removed.

I had always been very impressed by the Ingalls shipwrights. I believed all they ever needed was a management that would respect them, support them and give them a reasonable chance of success. I believed my work on Project X had played a role in providing them that chance.

Pat Keen, an Ingalls shipwright I had always respected, who had progressed through the Testing Department, was selected to be Vice

President of Operations. This was the Ingalls job I considered most important and the job to which I had always aspired. I envied him but knew he was the best person to lead the Ingalls' shipwrights.

I was told Pat had imposed the discipline essential to the "Shipyard of the Future" and had modified, as necessary, "Shipyard of the Future" procedures that had proved unwise. Ingalls became the reliable source of amphibious ships, cruisers and destroyers that the Navy and the Nation badly needed. Ingalls delivered 45 such ships to the Navy during the first decade following my move from Ingalls to Metro Machine including USS Ticonderoga in 1982.

Ticonderoga was one of the Navy's most important ships because it was the first to be equipped with the Aegis System, which provided an unprecedented capability to coordinate weapons of multiple ships.

Dad had played an early role in Aegis System development before he retired from APL in 1975. The Frank P. Goldbach Aegis System exhibit, which Janet and I sponsored, was the most important Nauticus exhibit.

I was especially proud that the Navy selected Metro Machine to perform the mid-life overhaul of USS Ticonderoga in the early 1990s. The Navy awarded Metro Machine a 100% performance fee score and its coveted Aegis Excellence Award, upon completing the overhaul.

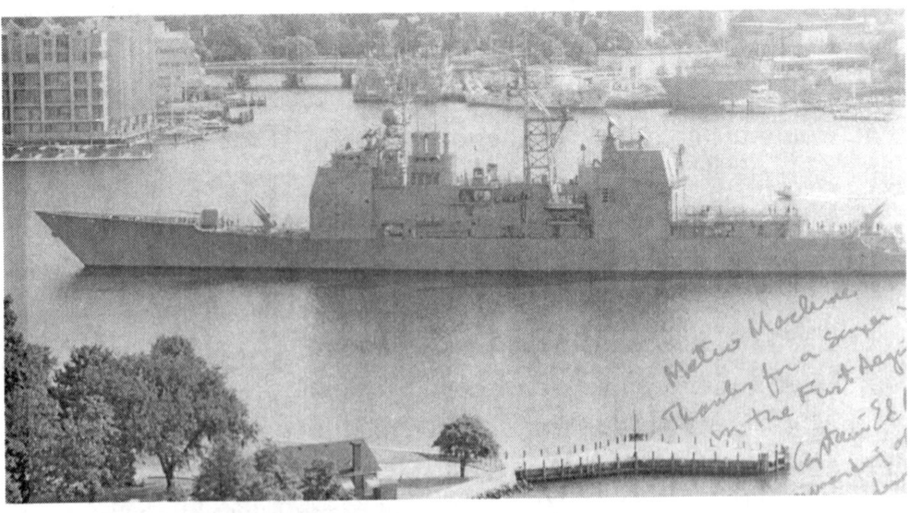

USS Ticonderoga departing Metro Machine

Pat Keen was awarded the William M. Kennedy Award by the Society of Naval Architects and Marine Engineers (SNAME), the honor SNAME gives each year to its most respected shipwright. He was to nominate me for the same award in 1997. When I received the award, the fact that Pat was the one who had nominated me meant more to me than the fact that I was chosen for the award.

My Project X saga was to include one more encounter with the book by Professor Ed Roberts that miraculously changed my life. While killing time one day in the Philadelphia Airport in the late 1990s, I came upon an old used copy in pristine condition that was for sale on a gurney for fifteen cents. Having seen enough of it for one lifetime, I called Ken Cooper to ask him if he wanted me to buy it for him. Ken agreed we should leave it on the gurney, although he did call Ed Roberts to tell him the miracles were continuing.

I wished there had been a way for me to find the owner of that fifteen-cent book so I could tell him how many hundreds of millions of dollars had been made by others based on just two pages of it.

4: *Tale of Systems Dynamics*

RICHARD GOLDBACH
MIT Legend

November 2011

Rich Goldbach is a legend in the field of system dynamics modeling and at MIT. He was the first to seek out SD modeling as a means of understanding complex project dynamics. He then guided the first project model's development with Ken Cooper's team at Pugh-Roberts--and guided it so clearly that the basics of that model design remain at the core of project modeling to this day and is used around the world, not only in the context of dispute resolution, but to improve project management so that both customer and contractor are pleased with the outcome.

Rich led the initial use of system dynamics at Ingalls to great success--technically (the first such model ever), commercially (yielding a large dispute resolution), and academically (the work became the first SD application to be a winner in the prestigious Edelman global award competition). He then carried those ideas even further in leading the people of Metro Machine to success for more than three decades.

Although I have never met Rich in person, he graciously shared the story of Metro with me by phone while I was writing my textbook. I recall vividly what he said about how the experience with modeling had affected him:

"For the [shipbuilding] industry I thought I was a pretty sophisticated manager, but it changed my whole perspective. I never had the ability I think I got from working with system dynamics to ask 'how will this decision ripple out?' I got to the point that I had the mental self-discipline to fight my impulses and not just do the macho thing when there's a problem.... Now I ask how customers, employees, suppliers and so on will react to what we might do. Sometimes I get it right and sometimes I don't, but it permeates every aspect of my thinking. I'm a different person than I was before."

Rich's story, and his intellectual contribution to the field, are now a permanent part of the lore of system dynamics, and they are discussed often in classrooms at MIT and around the world.

--Dr. John Sterman
Jay W. Forrester Professor of Management, Sloan School of Management
Massachusetts Institute of Technology

John is author of the definitive textbook on system dynamics, Business Dynamics. He leads the MIT system dynamics group, and is the global academic leader of the field.

5: Tale of Arrival at Metro Machine Shipyard 1977

I arrived at Metro Machine on April 2, 1977.

Without my thinking about it at the time, the me that arrived that day was the result of ten remarkable people unwittingly combining to prepare me to lead and provide for those that would choose to make their lives at Metro Machine.

Dad, Mom, William Webb and my teachers had taught me my lessons of life.

Janet had provided me inspiration, compassion and courage.

Al Zeien had taught me genius, Lloyd Bergeson had taught me organization and persistence, Norman McIntyre had taught me leadership.

Ken Cooper had given me a unique ability to look into the future.

Henry Swanner had given me his trust.

It was to turn out that Metro Machine success was going to require all I had inherited from them and much more.

I called a meeting of my new subordinates. After introducing myself to them, I faced them and asked,

"How many employees do we have?" After looking at a tab run, Dave McCoy replied, "86".

"How many workers do we have work for?" Dave didn't have to look this time. He said, "None".

"Whose job is it to get work?" Joe Gilbert, after clearing his throat said, "We all thought you were going to do that."

"Why don't we have any work?" Dave responded, "The Navy doesn't like us anymore."

"Why not?" Dave replied, "We miss schedules and they think our quality is poor."

In less than a minute, I had the job description that I would have for the next 34 years. It was: Never run out of work. Never run out of money. Keep the Navy liking us by Metro Machine meeting schedules and quality requirements.

I had no idea how to do any of those things. My job was to build a Metro Machine with people who would teach me how.

I picked up the phone and called Captain Bob Roach, Supervisor of Shipbuilding, Conversion and Repair, called SUPSHIP. He agreed to meet me that afternoon in his office.

When I got there, he added another complaint, "One of your vice presidents is suing me."

I said, "Thanks for giving me one easy one. But you're really going to like Metro Machine if you give us one more chance."

6: Tales of Henry's Shipyard Career

I published the following in the President's Corner of the July 1988 Metro Machine News:

"On June 12 of this year, Metro experienced the 25th anniversary of its founding. The event passed pretty much unnoticed here because of our preoccupation with current challenges and preparation for challenges yet to come.

While a few employees go back to the early days, no one who was in at the start of Metro is a current employee. The great majority of us came after 1977 when I did.

Most of you know Henry Swanner and know he was the founder of Metro. While I didn't meet Henry, or know of Metro until 1974 at the start of the negotiations to hire me as President, I'm going to use this month's newsletter to tell you what I know about the events that brought us this far. Everything earlier than 1977 is based on conversations with others so I hope those with different recollections will forgive any shortcomings.

Henry Swanner had been working with Moon Engineering for over twenty-three years. He was one of the better known and more highly respected machinists on the Norfolk waterfront. Many of Moon's customers asked for him by name when they needed work done.

I have heard many stories about Henry from people who knew him at Moon. Based on these stories, Henry often spoke about starting his own company. It seems no one ever took those statements seriously. According to Henry, his final decision to leave Moon and spend all his time on the new company came after a series of incidents when he became convinced his authority in assigning workers to jobs was being overridden. Perhaps others saw things differently, but right or wrong, these incidents succeeded in pushing Henry to make the decision he had long been considering....the decision that brought us here together.

Henry's company was started in a building at the Olney Road location next to the Midtown Tunnel where Mid Atlantic is today. The original building is no longer used by Metro. Original equipment was about six machine tools, purchased used. The original work force was made up of about six men, sometimes working part time, who knew Henry well enough to trust him with their futures. Henry's customers were NOAA, Tidewater Construction, Norfolk and Western, the Norfolk School System and various commercial customers who knew him and trusted him with their work.

After about a year, Henry decided he needed to bring someone in as a partner to handle the management side of the business, a side Henry's waterfront experience at Moon had not included. For some time, Henry had known and been discussing plans for his company with Walter Kelly, an engineer with Cottrell Engineering, which had offices upstairs from Moon. Walter came into Metro as an equal partner about one year after Henry started his company and, with Henry, applied for and received Metro's business license on June 12, 1963.

Little by little, through trial and error, the company began to follow the path which led it toward what it has become today. In 1966, Metro was granted its Master Ship Repair Contract with the United States Navy. This contract, which Metro still operates under, enabled Metro to compete for downriver work at NOB and Little Creek Navy Bases. This work built up to be the mainstay of the company's business until 1971. This MSR contract also enabled Metro in the late 1960s to successfully compete for the in-plant modification and repair of eleven small ATC gunboats.

It was largely the lucrative profits from this gunboat contract that Henry and Walter had in hand in the early 1970s during their search for a site which would permit Metro to undertake the in-plant topside (without drydocking) overhaul of larger Navy ships. The preferred site was the Berkley Shipyard where Old Dominion is located today. However, Metro's bid for the property was unsuccessful.

Ultimately in 1971, Walter and Henry purchased the Imperial Docks property for $700,000 cash. This purchase has to rank as one of the best bargains ever on the Norfolk waterfront. The Imperial Tobacco Company had, in the mid-1950s, spent $5 million on the sheet metal building expansion alone.

Metro immediately was awarded a contract for overhaul of the USS Francis Marion (LPA-249). I've heard many humorous stories about performing that major job at the same time the Imperial Docks were being modified with the minimum additions necessary for shipyard work. But the important fact is that Metro completed the job successfully.

The Francis Marion was followed by successful overhauls of USS Butte (AE-27) and USS El Paso (LKA-117). El Paso was followed by topside overhauls of USS Fort Snelling (LST-30) and USS Vulcan (AR-5)

Fort Snelling and Vulcan were significantly larger and more complex than Metro's earlier work. The ships were very old and in extremely poor condition. At the same time, a general Government investigation of the Norfolk waterfront was consuming much of the company's energy.

As a result of these and other factors, Metro's performance on Fort Snelling and Vulcan was not up to its performance on prior contracts. Navy representatives were dissatisfied and openly critical of Metro's performance. This resulted in Metro being removed from the Navy's bidders list for future in-plant topside overhauls for an indefinite period.

This series of events led Henry Swanner to conclude that Metro needed management for larger contracts and led ultimately to his deciding to hire me as President. My hiring was followed almost immediately by Henry's purchase of Walter Kelly's portion of Metro.

As Henry and I had our discussions, he repeatedly stated to me that, "We have people that can do the work, I just need someone who can manage them." This turned out to be accurate. Because of Henry's decision, the Navy gave Metro another chance on the in-plant availability of USS Caloosahatchee (AO-98). This job gave Metro the opportunity to start to implement the planning, material control and production control procedures necessary to successfully execute any large complex undertaking. The Navy commended Metro Machine's performance on the Caloosahatchee. This led to other opportunities on USS Recovery (ARS-43), USS Harlan County (LST-1196), USS Charleston (LKA-113) and USS Trenton (LPD-14)

By this time, in 1979, Metro had begun to receive recognition as one of the best east coast topside shipyards in the areas of quality and schedule performance. However, at the same time, the Navy was starting to conclude that it didn't have time in its overhaul schedules to have topside and drydock work done at separate shipyards. Opportunities for Metro to make topside bids were becoming scarce and individuals within the Navy were informally encouraging Metro to acquire a drydock.

Thus, Henry and I had to start contemplating acquiring a drydock in order to continue to compete for Navy overhaul work. We immediately found we were faced with two significant problems. While there were dry-

docks available for purchase, Metro had no place to put one and no money with which to buy one, even if it had the space.

The opportunity to solve the first problem soon came, but first, some background....Henry had never forgotten about his unsuccessful bid in 1970 on the Berkley shipyard, next to Metro. He mentioned it to me many times along with his conviction that, if we acquired it, that was all the land Metro would ever need. Henry did, in fact, try to negotiate its purchase on numerous occasions during the intervening years but all attempts failed. I wasn't convinced we needed the property but as the Navy started to change its overhaul policy, I came to realize Henry had been right all along.

Finally, in 1980, the Berkley Shipyard folded totally and had no one except Metro to turn to for a purchase of its property. After months of negotiations, Metro finally owned the property Henry had known from the beginning we needed

Next came the drydock. The search for a drydock and all the alternative exploration that went with that search took over a year. Once we found what we were looking for, negotiations took another year. Delivery and installation required six months after that.

Janet and Rich receive National Small Business Prime Contractor Award

In 1981, during these negotiations, Metro was selected as the National "Small Business Prime Contractor of the Year". The Small Business Administration awards this honor to the company it judges to be the best doing business with the federal Government. This award turned out to be instrumental in convincing the Banco Exterior of Spain to lend Metro the money needed to buy the Old Dominion Drydock it had selected in Spain.

Finally, In June 1982, we christened Old Dominion and placed it in service. But, for the first time in its history, Metro had a debt to pay off......seventeen million dollars' worth....and no Navy contract in sight. Then along came our old friend Caloosahatchee in the fall of 1982. This was Metro's first drydocking overhaul contract. Metro finished the Caloosahatchee drydock overhaul, its largest contract ever, ahead of schedule and under its bid cost. The "New" Metro was on its way.

Old Dominion Drydock arriving at Metro in May 1982

Rich greeting Old Dominion

Janet and Rich Mom, Dad, Rick, Kristen

Henry (R)

Old Dominion Christening June 12, 1982

Ironically, Metro's very first drydocking was for its archrival, Horne Brothers Shipyard. This was the USNS Comet operated by the Military Sealift Command. Metro's first Navy ship drydocking, USS Moinester (FF-1197) was also done for Horne Brothers which elected not to buy a drydock and, as a result went out of business in 1984 for lack of work.

Metro was the first shipyard in the Nation to offer drydock services to its competitors that didn't own drydocks. In addition to four drydockings done for Horne Brothers, Metro has done numerous drydockings for Jonathan Corporation, Allied Corporation and Norshipco. The results of this strategy largely offset the merchant ship drydockings projected when buying Old Dominion but lost because of the shipping industry depression of the 1980s.

Between 1983 and 1986, the Navy made major changes to the way it maintained its ships. Fewer and fewer regular overhauls, upon which Metro had depended, were scheduled. Phased maintenance was being implemented on all auxiliary and amphibious ships. Cruisers, destroyers and frigates, which had been overhauled in Naval shipyards, were competed between private shipyards using selected restricted availabilities requiring less work.

These new developments placed new demands on Metro's management, workforce and facilities. Phased maintenance required more people for advanced planning as well as additional office space to put those additional people in. In order to compete for its share of the work and provide a constant workload, Metro added piers to wet-berth four additional ships plus cranes for the piers and services for those additional ships and their crews. Crew berthing was expanded, and then expanded again. Office space for SUPSHIP (Supervisor of Shipbuilding, Conversion and Repair) was expanded to accommodate six teams of surveyors.

In 1984, Metro Machine began competing for the U.S. Navy's phased maintenance programs. Contracts for LSD-41 and LST ships were awarded in 1985. Contracts for LPH and LPD ships were awarded in 1986 bringing the number of ships to fourteen and making Metro the Nation's largest phased maintenance contractor. In 1986 and 1987, Metro expanded the capacity of Old Dominion to accommodate LPH, DD 963 and CG-47 ships.

USS Guam (LPH-9) on Old Dominion Drydock

Also, there are other aspects of acquiring Old Dominion Drydock which are discussed later in this section, I-10 "Community Partnering ." The acquisition revolutionized all aspects of Metro Machine.

By 1987, Metro had acquired a reputation within the Navy, as the premier shipyard in the Nation for quality and schedule performance repairing ships. Also, by 1987, Henry Swanner had seen everything done by his company that he had ever dreamed of. It seemed to be a good time to take the winnings of the gamble he had made twenty-five years previously and retire….the gamble no one except Henry thought he would win.

That's when the vision of the Metro Employees Stock Retirement Plan was born, the vision that will put almost all of the future benefits of Metro where it belongs….in the pockets of all employees whose experience, skills and innovation generates them. The vision permits not only participation in financial benefits unheard of in American Industry but also participation in the management process that generates those benefits….through the Weekly Employees Advisory Board and everyday teamwork toward achieving our common goals.

7: Tale of the 1987 Dream

The years following the 1977 handshake agreement between Henry and me flew by. I had told Henry I would find a way to buy him out in ten years. Yet because Metro Machine had grown in value so fast, I could see no way to do it.

It was time for another miracle!

Henry came to me one day and told me he was having discussions with investors looking to do a leveraged buyout of his stock. I was an engineer with no knowledge of such things, but I agreed to meet with any potential investors he brought to me.

When I did, I made several observations. First, none of these investors were prepared to risk much, if any, of their own money. Therefore, the primary risk that would be taken on any leveraged buyout was by the workers, who would incur a considerable risk of losing their jobs. Yet, they were not parties to the transaction and had no possibility of financial gain.

Second, the only investors approaching Henry had no ability to manage the complex work done by repair shipyards. Therefore, no investor speaking to Henry would buy Henry's stock unless I continued as CEO.

I refused to do so because I saw all risk in the deals going to the jobs of workers whose skills and efforts had created Metro Machine's value in the first place.

As I saw it, Henry and I had done some clever things that had been of significant financial benefit to the Company. But, all those clever things would have been for naught if we hadn't had production employees to do the difficult work that brought in the business.

I knew that, by the rules of Capitalism, financial risk trumps the risk of daily labors. But, Henry had risked only $10,000 originally and that seemed small compared to the livelihoods of 400 workers.

Also, the concept of investors, without operations management skills, taking out foolhardy loans and then running off with accumulated winnings earned by the sweat of loyal workers, was one I simply couldn't stomach, even to honor a commitment to a man I had come to love, a man who had saved me from failure.

There had to be a better way and that belief haunted me day and night. Then one night, during a sound sleep, a very complicated financial scheme miraculously came to me. I will never know where it came from because it involved a very complex transaction that no one had ever thought of before.

In the transaction, Metro Machine would borrow an amount of money from Virginia National Bank (VNB) equal to the amount it had paid off in the first five years of its Drydock loans. It would borrow a like amount from Henry Swanner with interest. Metro Machine would then use those loans to pay Henry his full asking price for his stock.

Janet and I would take the financial risk of increasing our personal loan guarantees to more than ten million dollars, even as our potential for investment gain remained comparable to that of all other employees. Henry would take the financial risk of making an unsecured loan of $8.5 million to the same workforce which had helped him build Metro Machine in the first place.

The employees would still be risking their jobs, but if they won that risk, they would receive all the profits Metro Machine made after 1986. My dream calculations indicated that, if the transaction was successful, Metro Machine would have more money after ten years if it bought Henry's stock than it would if it never bought Henry's stock and Henry remained owner.

The "dream" transaction would provide me a once-in-a-lifetime chance to be the absolute final authority of a potentially great shipyard. That was all I had hoped for since graduating from Webb Institute in 1958.

Every once in awhile, our lawmakers get something really right, even if they don't fully anticipate all the ways their legislation may ultimately be used! This was one of those times.

I got up in the middle of the night and wrote it all down so I wouldn't forget the details. But, there wouldn't be any more sleep for me that night. I got back up at 6:00 AM, grabbed my notes and headed for work.

At 7:00 AM, I called Marge Ryan, Metro Machine's Independent Accountant, at home and told her about my dream. She replied, "You can't do that."

I said, "I know, because it's too perfect. But tell me why."

Several hours later, Marge called back, all excited. "You can do it. It's a combination of approaches to an Employee Stock Ownership Plan (ESOP) that no one has ever used before."

Once we reduced my dream to paper, it took surprisingly little persuading of Metro Machine's Virginia National Bank (VNB) bankers to get them to approve VNB lending Metro Machine the $8.5 million needed. We were halfway through the payoff of our Old Dominion Drydock loans. VNB Chairman Cliff Cutchins, who had trusted me five years earlier by approving the Old Dominion loan, trusted me again.

By the end of Metro Machine's fiscal year on September 1, 1987, the new Metro Machine ESOP owned all of Henry's stock. Henry had over $8.5 million in cash and was out from under any financial risk. He had trusted the skills and hard work of his former workers to pay him another $8.5 million. The Metro Machine ESOP had received its first $5 million payment from Metro Machine profits.

It had taken me just 10 years and five months after my arrival at the Metro Machine gate to meet my commitment to buy all of Henry's stock in 10 years. Henry's 1963 investment of $10,000 was worth another $17 million.

I was named sole trustee for the stock owned by the ESOP, making me the only shipyard manager in the Nation with complete control of his/her company's decision making. When added to the extraordinary shipyard skills I inherited from my three original shipyard mentors, the lessons of life from my parents and teachers, the inspiration I received from Janet and the ability to predict the future I learned from Ken Cooper; that pretty much made me Superman.

But, I couldn't ever lose the trust of the employee-owners, because that trust was absolutely essential for me to achieve ESOP success.

25 years and 2months later, I distributed stock valued at 165 million dollars to the roughly 400 employees of Metro Machine. Everyone had their money by September 1, 2017. I could finally stop being Superman.

8: *Tales of Caring for Workers*

One of the biggest problems I had to contend with as Director of Division Planning of Ingalls Shipbuilding was extraordinary turnover of production workers. One year we started with almost 20,000 workers, hired an additional 20,000 workers but wound up with fewer than 100 more than at the start of the year. Systems Dynamics clearly showed that this turnover had a devastating effect on Ingalls' worker efficiency, although I intuitively knew that anyway.

Soon after I arrived in Norfolk, I realized Metro Machine and the other Norfolk shipyards also had a high turnover rate. I came to suspect that this high turnover rate was caused by hourly workers in the port having no loyalty to their employers because they were convinced their employers had no loyalty to them. I believed it would help Metro Machine compete if the turnover was significantly reduced.

I noticed that workers flocked to Metro when it was working a lot of overtime only to leave when the overtime reduced. This was called "following the overtime."

The solution to this problem at Metro Machine was so simple I never could understand why no other Norfolk shipyard ever did what I did. I simply implemented three automatic longevity increases every eighteen months for workers with continuous service. Workers no longer left when overtime was reduced because they returned to "Go" whenever they came back.

Metro Machine worker loyalty, with all its significant benefits, improved immediately, and then improved again with Metro Machine's vastly improved medical plan. The cost of the longevity increases was insignificant compared to the well-established benefits of improved worker loyalty.

When I assumed the job of Metro Machine CEO in 1977, overall compensation of Metro Machine workers paid by monthly salary included Blue Cross and Blue Shield (BC/BS) insurance. However, overall compensation of workers paid by the hour did not include the cost of any medical insurance and most hourly workers chose not to purchase medical insurance. Therefore, they and their families were uninsured. Metro Machine offered no employee dental insurance.

Metro Machine's addition of large drydock repair capability in 1982 brought with it a demand for a larger, more skilled and more stable workforce. This led to my re-examining the approach to providing medical care that would be best for retaining all these essential workers. It seemed to me that all workers would become more loyal to Metro Machine if the company showed it cared enough for them to pay not only their medical expenses, but also those of their families.

From my start as Metro CEO, I had always expressed a strong interest in the approach that BC/BS used to establish Metro Machine rates during annual policy renewals. The BC/BS approach to computing each proposed follow-year rate involved BC/BC quoting a factor for administrative/handling fees, projected escalation and profit. This factor was then multiplied by Metro Machine's actual incurred prior-year medical costs to determine the renewal price.

As I recall, the factor applied was generally around 60%. I concluded from this that, if Metro Machine avoided medical insurance and paid medical providers directly, the savings would provide most of the money needed to provide medical insurance to those Metro Machine workers paid hourly as well as those paid by monthly salary.

I suspected that medical providers might be reluctant to risk making such a dramatic change for a customer as small as Metro Machine, because it might negatively affect their relationships with their biggest insurance company customers. Those big insurance companies might well suspect that Metro Machine's medical providers were trying to steal big insurance company customers.

To overcome any medical provider reluctance, I decided to offer additional inducements to Metro Machine's medical providers. One of these was to agree that each medical provider contracted with, would receive all the business Metro Machine would generate in their specialty, thereby increasing their sales.

A second was to eliminate the enormous quantity of paperwork the medical insurance providers were requiring the medical providers to submit to them to justify payment. Instead, Metro Machine would promptly pay any and all medical provider bills that included certification that the medical procedure rates charged were consistent with medical provider rates charged other best customers. This enormous amount of paperwork required by insurance companies had been delaying medical provider cash flow by up to a year as well as causing medical providers to incur excessive administrative costs.

I first approached Dr. James Carty, my own internist, with this proposition. Dr. Carty worked with a sizeable number of other physicians in an organization named Norfolk Diagnostic Clinic or NDC which was highly regarded and located in a place convenient to all Metro Machine employees. NDC also had needed relationships with Leigh Memorial Hospital and Norfolk General Hospital, both considered among the best hospitals in the Tidewater, Virginia area.

It took NDC, Leigh and Norfolk General six months to respond positively to my offer. Once they did, they assisted Don Fisher, Metro Machine V.P. of Human Resources, to fill out the required Metro Machine stable of medical providers. In another six months, the Metro Machine medical program was in full swing, where it would stay for over two decades until implementation of the Affordable Care Act. Largely because of NDC's arrangement with Metro Machine, NDC was able to implement the region's first Urgent Care Facility, which has now successfully served Metro Machine and many other clients for over 25 years.

The Metro Machine employee-owner side of each medical transaction was made just as simple as the medical provider side. Employee-owners and their family members were automatically enrolled in the program after 30 days of employment at Metro Machine, at no cost to them. To receive medical care, all they had to do was show up at the medical provider and be on the list of those qualified to receive Metro Machine medical care.

As Metro Machine received the medical provider bills for the medical care employees and/or family members, 10% (outpatient) and 20% (inpatient) of the cost was deducted from the employee's paycheck as a co-pay. However, no single paycheck could ever be reduced by more than 10%.

Employees who chose to compete for healthy lifestyle co-pay rates, which were 5% (outpatient) and 10% (inpatient), could do so if they complied with designated body fat, blood pressure, mammogram, smoking and illegal drug criteria. Metro Machine employee co-pay amounts were capped at $2000 per employee per year. Hardship concessions were the rule rather than the exception.

During most of the 25-year period of Metro Machine employee ownership, until implementation of the Affordable Care Act, all Metro Machine employees and their family members received this Metro Machine medical care. This care was judged by them and the Tidewater, Virginia medical provider industry to be the very best available in the region.

To implement this extraordinary employee medical program, Metro Machine contracted directly with the single Tidewater, Virginia provider in each medical specialty that it determined to be the best in that specialty. This saved Metro Machine all cost of the insurance company itself, generating savings that Metro Machine instead used for improving and expanding employee medical care. Also, I was convinced that exclusively using the most capable medical providers would save the company money from medical rework, just as Metro Machine saved the Navy money because of its superior quality and its negligible rework.

Employee dental care was provided by employing on-site, a single full-time dentist, with no staff. This employed dentist, retired from the Navy, was capable of performing all but the most unique dental procedures, such as implants. These were contracted out, with the employee repayment limited to Metro Machine's own cost. The Metro Machine Dentist was capable of performing root canals and crowns, which cost the employee little or nothing if it required less than one hour in the dentist chair.

A fully-equipped modern dental facility was installed in the Personnel Office, convenient to all work-sites. Each employee and each employee family member was entitled to one hour in the dental chair every six months. Employee and family member time in the dental chair was free to each employee. Employees received their regular pay whenever they were in the dental facility.

Metro Machine's total cost for providing dental care in this manner was insignificant compared to what the cost would have been if Metro Machine had instead purchased traditional dental insurance. Payment of the insurance company component of traditional dental insurance was completely avoided, enabling all dental care funds to be used for the cost of providing dental care itself.

Perhaps most important, whenever an employee or dependent didn't show up for their bi-annual dental care, they received a call from Dr. Haydu, Metro Machine's dentist. He made sure every Metro Machine Employee and their dependents had good teeth. He even sneaked in grandkids and unrelated neighbor kids whenever he could fit them in his schedule.

9: Tales of Teaching Workers

Every Navy warship is more complex than a small city. The repair and modernization work package of every ship is different from that of every other ship. Therefore, the worker skills used in ship repair are numerous and enormously varied. Meanwhile the number of workers employed by individual shipyards is usually in the 100s. Metro Machine averaged 500 to 1000 workers, including contract workers.

Specialized skill training of repair shipwrights is therefore not best done by the individual shipyards themselves. It is best done by teaching specialized skills required by workers of individual shipyards in combination with specialized skills of workers of other industries, and/or other shipyards. I believed employee training in repair shipyards was best accomplished by making use of outside training organizations which have access to broad expertise.

Therefore, my approach to training of the Metro Machine employee-owners was to assure I was knowledgeable of the training opportunities already available from publicly supported training organizations. Additionally, I also made sure publicly supported training organizations were knowledgeable of and responsive to the needs of Metro Machine.

This I did by playing a very influential role in two very competent publicly supported worker training organizations. One was the Tidewater Maritime Training Institute (TMTI), which I founded, and the other, Tidewater Community College (TCC), where I served as the Norfolk Board Member. During my time on the Board, I pushed through creation of a Norfolk campus to complement the Chesapeake, Portsmouth and Virginia Beach campuses while concentrating on shipwright skills training.

TMTI was generally used for training workers possessing no learned skills to become semi-skilled shipyard workers. TCC was used for teaching workers highly specialized skills such as hazardous waste processing.

UNANIMOUS RESOLUTION BY THE
BOARD OF DIRECTORS OF THE TIDEWATER
MARITIME TRAINING INSTITUTE, INC.

WHEREAS, the Tidewater Maritime Training Institute, Inc. (the "Institute") was organized for the purpose of the development and operation of a training facility for the ship repair industry in Tidewater, Virginia; and

WHEREAS, the Institute and its members have been directly involved in and largely responsible for the successful formation and operation of the Tidewater Maritime Training Center (the "Center"); and

WHEREAS, the establishment of the Institute required skillful management and coordination by its Board of Directors; and

WHEREAS, the Board of Directors for the Institute chose Mr. Richard A. Goldbach as its President to provide leadership in the formative stages of both the Institute and the Center; and

WHEREAS, Richard A. Goldbach successfully achieved the difficult task of gaining the cooperation and positive support of fourteen independent, private sector shipyards/ship repair facilities who comprised the Institute; and

WHEREAS, Richard A. Goldbach gave of his time, energy and talents to direct and monitor an organization that has gained the respect of the civic and business community in Tidewater, Virginia; and

WHEREAS, he provided a suitable training site for the Maritime Training Center at no cost to the funding sponsors; and

WHEREAS, he encouraged and fully supported the Center's staff in the training of some one hundred and sixty graduates of the Center; and

WHEREAS, he gave many hours of his professional time in personal discussions with, and in behalf of, seven graduating classes from the Center; and

WHEREAS, he fostered a receptive and positive attitude in the Institute for a Center that was nationally exemplary in the proper use of federal training dollars and private sector employment; and

WHEREAS, his personal involvement in the Institute resulted in the unsubsidized employment in private sector shipyards of ninety percent of the Center's graduates; and

WHEREAS, the Center's graduates have performed well in entry level positions at various ship repair facilities thus contributing to repair yard productivity and to the local population tax base;

NOW, THEREFORE, BE IT RESOLVED, that the Board of Directors for the Tidewater Maritime Training Institute, in full concert, recognize the contribution of its President, Richard A. Goldbach, to the Institute's remarkable progress during the period February 1982 to February 1983; and

BE IT FURTHER RESOLVED, that the Board of Directors extend to Richard A. Goldbach their grateful appreciation for his outstanding performance.

I certify that the foregoing resolution was unanimously approved by the Directors of the Tidewater Maritime Training Institute, Inc., at its duly called meeting on March 10, 1983.

Thomas C. Atkins

Secretary

Resolution

TIDEWATER COMMUNITY COLLEGE

Whereas, Richard A. Goldbach was appointed to the Tidewater Community College Board and has served as an active member representing the city of Norfolk since July 1983, and

Whereas, Richard A. Goldbach will complete two full terms on the Tidewater Community College Board in 1991, and

Whereas, Richard A. Goldbach did serve as treasurer of the Tidewater Community College Board, and

Whereas, Richard A. Goldbach did serve as Vice Chairman of the Tidewater Community College Board, and

Whereas, Richard A. Goldbach did serve as a member of the Building and Site Committee and chairman of the Building and Site Committee, and

Whereas, Richard A. Goldbach did serve Tidewater Community College faithfully and well in all positions he held on the Tidewater Community College Board, and

Whereas, Richard A. Goldbach performed with honesty, efficiency, and insight, and

Whereas, Richard A. Goldbach is held in high esteem and respect by the Tidewater Community College Board,

Now, Therefore, be it resolved that the Tidewater Community College Board, assembled this Graduation Day, May 12, 1991, expresses its sincere gratitude to Richard A. Goldbach for his valuable services to Tidewater Community College and extends its very best wishes to him.

CHAIRMAN, TIDEWATER COMMUNITY COLLEGE BOARD

CHAIRMAN, TRANSITION MANAGEMENT TEAM

10: Tales of Community Partnering

I first encountered Dr. Mason Andrews in 1981, soon after I had acquired the dilapidated seven acre Berkley Shipyard adjacent to the original Metro Machine property. I had just bought the shipyard to accommodate the Old Dominion Drydock that I planned to acquire in Madrid. The Berkley Shipyard had a problem: the famous Schooner Atlantic had capsized at one of its piers and no one knew how to remove it without destroying what still remained of it.

Removal and disposal of Atlantic in a respectful manner was deemed to be very important. Despite its deplorable condition, the Atlantic was still the flagship of the New York Yacht Club because it still held the record, set in 1905, for an eastern crossing of the Atlantic Ocean under sail. The record time was 12 days, 4 hours, 1 minute and 19 seconds. Some of the famous millionaires who had sailed on Atlantic as children were still alive. Many, for sentimental reasons, wanted a piece of the Atlantic and were prepared to use any influence they had to get it.

I was sitting in my office one day when Jim Frazier, Metro Machine General Superintendent, came in to tell me there was a group looking at the three Atlantic masts. I dashed out just as they were leaving. I stopped the last uninvited visitor as he was climbing into his car and said, "Who are you and what are you doing?" He said, "I'm with Dr. Andrews to help him pick out the Atlantic mast he wants to erect in the new Towne Point Park." I said, "But those masts aren't his, they're mine." He said, "That doesn't matter to Dr. Andrews." Then he climbed the rest of the way into his car and drove off, following the others.

This really made me scratch my head. I didn't really care who got the masts because I was going to have to get rid of them anyway. Dr. Andrews' possibly excessive zeal with the masts would certainly never have been considered to be a shortcoming by shipwrights.

I just needed to show Dr. Andrews who the real boss was.

I went over to Towne Point Park, which was still under construction by the City of Norfolk and found the site which looked like the only place the mast could go. Only one of the three Atlantic masts

Dr. Andrews had been looking at seemed suitable for that site. Metro Machine workers made welding repairs to that mast, then abrasive blasted and painted it. The next night, after dark, I went over with a few carefully selected workers and welded the renovated mast onto the likely site, complete with a plaque which I had fabricated overnight, glorifying the Atlantic and Metro Machine.

Around noon, I received the expected call from City Hall. "Who said you could install that mast?" Answer: "Nobody" Question: You didn't have a permit. Take it down." Answer: If you want it down, take it down yourself. But don't ask me for help putting it back up." CLICK

It was fun to fight City Hall that one time and be willing to pay the price. The mast stayed up for 10 years. Then I had Metro Machine workers remove it because I feared the corrosion on the 75-year-old steel was beginning to create a safety hazard for passers-by.

Even after those 10 years, I was just beginning to know Norfolk's extraordinary Dr. Mason Andrews.

I was an engineer and shipwright in 1982. I knew a lot about drydocks and how to operate them. I had never dealt as much with banks as most businessmen had.

After 1977, I became the Metro Machine shipwright whose job it was to make sure Metro Machine never ran out of money and the Metro Machine workforce never ran out of work. Metro consistently satisfied the Navy after I arrived in 1977. Therefore, Metro Machine had not run out of work or money since then.

A time came in 1982 when the Navy advised me that Metro Machine would need a drydock if it was to continue to serve the Navy on Navy pier-side ship maintenance. That meant Metro Machine was going to run out of work for its workers if it didn't buy one soon. Unfortunately, Metro Machine buying a drydock in 1982 required a lot of money that Metro Machine didn't have.

I first sought the advice of Rob, my twin, on how to find a drydock. Rob bought, sold and operated ships for a living. He was very good at it. He said I had better use a ship broker when acquiring any marine vessel. He recommended Howard Yaffee, a Michigan Naval Architect living in Florida.

Howard soon found the perfect drydock for the U.S. Navy ships worked by Metro Machine. But the price for the drydock Howard found was ten times the amount of money Metro Machine had.

I called Rob and asked him if he had any idea where Metro Machine could borrow the money needed to buy the drydock. He gave me the names of two New York bankers he did business with. They agreed to meet with me. How hard could it be? I flew to New York with a briefcase full of papers.

Each banker gave me three to five minutes in the lobby. I didn't get inside of the office of either. They both dismissed me abruptly, saying the same thing: "It's not bankable." I had no idea what they meant.

I was humiliated and thought I had probably embarrassed Rob. I flew back to Norfolk and had lunch at the Omni Hotel with John Matson, the Bank of Virginia V. P. responsible for Metro Machine's checking and deposit accounts. What does "not bankable" mean John? He said, "A bank won't touch it."

Well, that was a start. I asked, "What will they touch?" He responded, "If you get the Spanish Government to lend you most of the money, you might get a local bank to lend you the rest." "Now we're talking," I thought.

I called Howard Yaffee and said, "We need Spanish Government financing of our drydock." After checking, he came back with the advice that 80% financing at 1/3 of prime was available to qualified buyers. "You're going to need a business plan that convinces Banco Exterior, the lender, that you have the other 20 percent of the drydock purchase price, the funds to pay for installing the drydock and the ability to pay off the 80 percent borrowed."

The first part was the easiest. I knew we could get enough Navy work to pay for the dock. I was always good at numbers, like my Dad. Besides, Marge Ryan, our independent accountant, had been nagging me to work with her on a Metro Machine business plan anyway. I had been operating without one.

Just in time to fund the other 20 percent of the Old Dominion purchase price, the Reagan tax cuts were passed. They had an initial provision that investors could sell the Reagan tax benefits to others if they didn't have enough income to use them themselves. The provision used to sell tax benefits was a financial instrument called a Safe Harbor Lease. I knew nothing about it.

Soon thereafter, a lawyer new to me happened to come to talk to me about the Schooner Atlantic and its possible value. While there, he said he had heard I was interested in finding a Safe Harbor Lease partner. He gave me a name and a telephone number with a Kentucky area code. I called the number and asked for the person. I was told they needed some time to get him because he was down at the barn. I hung on the phone for half an hour waiting for him.

When he finally came to the phone, he told me he owned race horses and was doing several race horse Safe Harbor Leases with Potomac Electric Power Company (Pepco). He surely made race horses sound more interesting than drydocks. He gave me a name to call at Pepco.

Soon afterward, I called that name. Pepco agreed to buy Metro Machine's surplus tax benefits for $3 million. Suddenly, Metro Machine had the funds it needed for its twenty percent drydock deposit!

That still left the need for a $3 million loan for mooring, dredging and electrical power costs associated with installing the drydock on the Berkley Shipyard. The only possible source for such a loan was a local bank. Metro Machine had no collateral to offer since drydock installation costs wouldn't contribute to the distress sale value of the Berkley Shipyard.

I had already been discussing my need for this loan with loan officers of all the local banks. But, I had been unable to generate any sincere banker interest. Only one of them, Virginia National Bank (VNB), was considered substantial enough to consider taking a risk like that with a small business company like Metro Machine.

Bob McMillan, Metro Machine's consulting lawyer at the time, offered to try to set up a meeting for me with Mr. Cliff Cutchins, VNB Chairman. Cliff Cutchins was a legendary Virginia banker, of whom every Tidewater, Virginia businessman stood in awe. Mr. Cutchins agreed to meet with me, which seemed to surprise everyone who knew both of us.

My enthusiastic presentation of the Metro Machine story appeared to entertain Mr. Cutchins. At the end of our meeting, he grinned and turned to Doyle Hull, Norfolk's most powerful banker, and said "Make sure Rich gets what he needs." Sadly, today's bankers cannot make decisions based on the kind of character judgement Cliff Cutchins made that day.

I didn't hear from Doyle after that day. The day eventually came when Astilleros Espanoles, the builder and owner of the drydock Howard Yaffee had found, advised it would hold it for only two more days. We were virtually out of time.

I called Doyle repeatedly but he did not return my calls. I verified he was in the bank. Finally, I drove across the Berkley Bridge and camped out at the bottom of the bank of elevators that was Doyle's only way out of VNB. I scanned every face exiting each of the six elevators for over an hour.

Finally, Doyle came down with two other men. I took his arm in mine and walked him back into the elevator saying, "Let's go back up to the Harbor Club and talk about what Cliff Cutchins said to you". I wasn't even a member of the Harbor Club, but I knew Doyle had to be one!

I've often thought that I may have been the only business person in Virginia that day who would have done that. But, I knew I had to!

The Rickover witch hunt Government lawyers had nothing on Doyle that night. After hours of intense interrogation, Doyle agreed to give me the notification Banco Exterior demanded. I silently thanked Admiral Rickover for preparing me for that night.

Concluding the conversation, Doyle said, "Oh by the way, you and your wife will have to guarantee the loan, even though you won't own any part of the drydock." There was no consideration of backing out. That night was the start of Janet and me personally guaranteeing all Metro Machine loans for the next twenty-seven years.

Howard and I immediately planned to fly to Madrid the next day to meet with top executives of Banco Exterior.

There was a City of Norfolk business certification I needed Mayor Joe Leafe to provide me to give to Banco Exterior. While I was at City Hall, Joe said, "Let me give you the keys to the City of Norfolk. Mayors are actually respected in Europe." With Marge's hastily prepared business plan, a picture of me together with President Reagan at our Small Business Prime Contractor of the Year award, a safe harbor lease letter from Pepco, the VNB letter and the keys to the City of Norfolk in my briefcase, Janet drove me to the Norfolk Airport to fly to Kennedy Airport and then to Madrid.

As Janet was dropping me off at the Norfolk airport, she said, "I'm sure you have your passport for your New York flight to Madrid, but I just have to ask." Of course, I didn't! Janet raced home to get my passport in time for me to board the plane to Kennedy Airport. I've often wondered what would have happened to all of us through the following years if Janet had not gotten my passport to me on my plane to Kennedy Airport.

There ought to be a place reserved on every man's tombstone for the message, "He had a wife who always pulled his chestnuts out of the fire." I can't think of anything any husband ever needed that was more important than Janet's reminder to me that day!

Janet's getting me on that plane with a passport was the final thing I needed. The keys to the City of Norfolk made a hit. Our application for financing was approved. Minutes after Astilleros Espanoles executed an agreement to sell its drydock to Metro Machine based on that financing, a Spanish lawyer came in waving a Chinese offer. It was $3 million higher than Metro Machine's just executed contract, without the need for the financing included in Metro's contract. Henry's trust in me had enabled me to beat the Chinese Shipyard by minutes!

"With no money, no business education or experience, and no investment education or experience, I had bought and installed a brand new 15,000 ton lift floating drydock with a mortgage at 30% of prime rate." I was to repeat that statement many times in the future to the many overzealous folks who called to induce me into "Can't Miss" schemes. It would always save a lot of conversation.

If I had known in advance all I would ultimately need to do during my drydock episode, I would probably have concluded it wasn't possible and wasn't worth my time. I look on this episode as evidence that success is based as much on how you make your way through the situations you find yourself in, as it is on the wisdom of your decisions.

Everyone who eventually joined me on my adventures would

have lived a very different life if any part of my drydock search had turned out differently. Few of them had any knowledge of what I was up to at the time.

Howard Yaffee was as tenacious as I was! As a result of this single transaction, Howard would become the Go-To U.S. Ship Broker For Floating Drydocks for 35 years. Not bad for a University of Michigan Naval Architect! He was to broker the extraordinary Metro Machine transactions for repair of Old Dominion Drydock in 2000 and acquisition of Speede Drydock in 2002. Both of these were indispensable to Metro Machine survival.

While there were still huge problems to be encountered after 1982, that was really that – except for one thing, which seemed minor at the time. About two years later, I received a direct call from Mr. Cutchins. He said, "How's your drydock coming, Rich?" I answered, "Great, sir - thanks to you."

He said, "Good, because I'd like to ask a little favor. The Norfolk Chamber of Commerce asked me to give them a candidate for their Board of Directors and it seems that that's something you'd enjoy." I said, "What's the Chamber of Commerce, sir?" He replied, "It's a bunch of business folks that get together and talk." "Right up my alley," I said.

I was surprised several years later to be chosen as the next Norfolk Chamber of Commerce Chairman. It seems they had assumed my assertiveness in meetings meant I cared about the outcome. In fact, it was just me being a shipwright. Nonetheless, I was truly complimented by their choice and was pleased to serve, despite knowing there were many others far more qualified for the job.

One of the more interesting aspects of being Norfolk Chamber of Commerce Chairman was also being a member of the Mayor's Downtown Development Committee, the organization that was most influential with the important Downtown Norfolk rebuilding efforts. Even though I had little to bring to commercial development, I found it very interesting to listen to some really knowledgeable individuals discuss such an interesting subject.

One thing was very clear, it was Dr. Mason Andrews' Committee, whether he was Mayor or not and normally he was not. While most of the ideas came from the group, Mason knew when to stop talking and get it done. It was easy to see how the extraordinary Norfolk Downtown progress that had taken place since my 1977 arrival had occurred. No wonder he had outsmarted me on the Atlantic mast!

The City of Norfolk had been holding discussions with Jacques Cousteau since before my 1977 arrival in Norfolk. It hoped to locate the Cousteau Center in downtown Norfolk to meet the recognized need of a tourist magnet attraction there. The residents and media seemed quite taken by the idea.

I had no involvement in these discussions. But, I had a strong impression that Jacques Cousteau and his son made it very difficult for the City to negotiate whenever the Cousteau objectives needed to be compromised with those of the City of Norfolk.

One morning before the Downtown Development Committee meeting, Mayor Joe Leafe made a major public announcement. Norfolk had cut off the ten year long discussions with Jacques Cousteau and would pursue other unnamed tourist magnet attraction possibilities.

Naturally, Downtown Committee members were a bit unsettled as they discussed the matter in their regular meeting. The Cousteau Center had been an important part of Downtown Norfolk planning for a decade. Mason Andrews recommended quickly appointing a chairman to plan a replacement attraction. Typically, I said nothing.

After the meeting, the attendees departing the meeting were waiting for the elevator to reach the 11th floor conference level. Just to make conversation, I said, "I never understood why we were talking to Jacques Cousteau in the first place. Norfolk is not a recognized center of environmental expertise."

I noticed everyone was looking at me as the elevator arrived, the door opened and we walked in. So, I continued, "but Norfolk is the most important center of maritime activity in the world." As the door closed, and the elevator descended floor by floor, I started to tick off, "the biggest navy fleet in the world, one of the biggest container shipping ports in the world, the biggest construction shipyard in the world, the most important Naval shipyard in the world, one of the biggest coal ports in the world, the Coast Guard, the Largest Navy Base in the

World, the National Oceanic and Atmospheric Administration and the Weather Channel."

When the elevator reached the ground floor and the doors opened, Mason Andrews stepped out saying, "I think we just selected our Chairman." No one else said anything. Off he walked without saying another word.

Several days later, without anyone ever discussing the matter with me, I was advised that I had been named by City Council to be Chairman of the attraction, which eventually was named Nauticus.

Working with the leading minds of Norfolk on all the complex demands of this project for three years was a delight. One of the most astute of these leading minds was retired Vice Admiral "Jack" Parker, ex-Navy Mayor of Norfolk and my friend. Jack served ex-officio on the Chamber Board when I did. Jack worked with me as Nauticus Executive Director until his death from Cancer just before Nauticus opened.

Janet and I were pleased to sponsor one of the major Nauticus Navy exhibits in Jack's name. I was also pleased that Janet and I could sponsor the Frank P. Goldbach Aegis Theater, one of the premier attractions of Nauticus, especially because Dad was in on the Navy's important Aegis program from its inception.

When Nauticus opened, my twin brother Rob and Al Eaton, Dad's ex-boss and best friend from the Johns Hopkins Applied Physics Laboratory (APL), were there with their wives. At my request and with Navy approval, APL had provided technical consultation for the Aegis exhibit.

Nauticus far exceeded my expectations as a maritime technology attraction, although I was disappointed that I did not reach the fundraising goals I had agreed to meet. Cliff Cutchins came to my rescue one more time after he retired from VNB. He agreed to serve as Chairman of the Nauticus Foundation. I was to witness again what an extraordinary gentleman he was.

Nauticus and working with the great minds of Norfolk was a labor of love. But the greatest of these great minds was my highly respected new friend, Dr. Mason Andrews. My thoughts turned to him one Christmas in the late 1990s.

I was overwhelmed as I drove through the beautiful city Mason Andrews' vision, persistence and energy had produced in just 20 years. I just had to send him a letter letting him know how I felt. I will always treasure his response.

From the City of Norfolk/Mason Andrews to Rich January 4, 1999

"Dear Rich,

Your note of December 28 is one of the very best things that has happened to me during this holiday season and, in fact, forever.

It was eloquently expressed, I hope somewhat perceptive, very nourishing, and deeply appreciated. As you observed, progress in un-pioneered fields depends on the brains and commitment of many people.

I can remember as far back as the days of identifying the need for a community college in Norfolk that you were the earliest and most perceptive and effective advocate. This was one of many areas in which you were an important part of the team and continue to be. Nauticus is an indispensable part of the entire picture and one of the reasons why the hotels are full and others are forming.

Over the years one of the great rewards for expending my energies in this way has been the ability to know and work with the quality of people which you represent and which were involved in one way or another with planning and implementing downtown and the medical school. Some, such as Phil Hammer, got paid for their work, but what they gave was far more than what they got paid for because of the skills which they possessed and decided to assign to our projects. I believe the type of people here that was working on them were one of the reasons why people such as Phil Hammer, Ray Gindroz, Jim Rouse and Vincent Kling chose to direct their energies here. The voluntarily contributed participation of local leaders was the indispensable element in Norfolk, Baltimore, and Philadelphia.

Thank you so much for taking the time to share your very nourishing thoughts. We hope you will continue to have involvement in the economic and civic life of this community and contribute your very valuable capabilities. Sabine joins me in sending our admiration and appreciation.

With best wishes for the new year,
Sincerely,

Mason C. Andrews, M.D."

Mason Andrews and Metro Machine's marriage to the City of Norfolk were on my mind when I prepared my 2002 remarks for the dedication of Metro Machine's new Speede Norfolk Drydock. Speede had been installed hundreds of feet from and in clear sight of the beautiful new Downtown Norfolk.

"Thank you Mayor Fraim for speaking to the employee-owners, families and friends of Metro Machine on this extraordinary occasion, the dedication of Speede Drydock, the most modern drydock in the World.

Last night, as I was looking forward to today on the drive from the airport to the Sheraton, my thoughts went back to a similar trip in 1975.

Bingo Stant, a Norfolk lawyer who had an office in what is now the Bank of America Building, had told me about Metro Machine in 1973. Bingo's clients included both Metro Machine and Ingalls Shipbuilding in Mississippi, where I was working at the time.

Bingo really liked Henry Swanner, Metro's founder and owner and wanted me to get together with him. Two years later in October 1975, that get-together was finally taking place on a return trip from one of my Washington meetings.

I remember asking the clerk at the Airport Hertz counter how to get to the Omni Hotel, where I was to spend my first-ever night in Norfolk. She said to turn right on I-264 until you see the tall buildings and then turn left. Last night, 27 years later, I followed the exact same route.

I remember the comfort and newness of the Omni Hotel and its location right on the Norfolk waterfront. I remember the view out my hotel window, which turned out to be the Metro Machine Imperial Docks with USS Fort Snelling alongside. Bingo Stant's Virginia National Bank Building office right across Waterside Drive had the same view of Metro Machine when I visited him after my arrival.

I remember walking through downtown Norfolk, which had a handful of municipal and bank buildings in the middle of an otherwise worn out area. One of the new buildings was the Scope Municipal Auditorium, where I went that same night to see the third Ali-Frazier fight on closed circuit TV. That fight sure lived up to its "Thrilla-in-Manila" promise.

Today, the rebuilding of downtown Norfolk, which was barely start-

ed when I visited in 1975, is now all but complete. North of the Eastern Branch of the Elizabeth River, City and civic-minded leaders have succeeded in adding world-class residential neighborhoods, restaurants, entertainment facilities, tourist attractions, higher –education facilities, arts facilities, retail establishments, hospital buildings, parking facilities, hotels and commercial office buildings.

The planning, political action and financial risk it took to achieve Norfolk's revitalized downtown will benefit all of Norfolk's private and business residents for the decades of the 21st Century. Prospects for jobs will be better, schools will be better and personal security will be better.

But when we look at Norfolk's new downtown buildings and roads, we don't see the real rewards the buildings have brought.

We don't see the welfare mom who can finally hold her family together because she landed a sales job at Nordstrom's.

We don't see the ten-year old boy who proudly reads to his unemployed father, who can't read.

We don't see the secretary who doesn't get mugged as she walks to her parked car after a long day's work.

We don't see any of the social problems that aren't there anymore, thanks to the energy and wisdom of Norfolk's citizen-leaders.

Except for the time it takes hot water to reach my sixth-floor shower, the Sheraton today is just as good today as the Omni was 27 years ago. But then, except for the time it takes my blood to circulate, I'm also just as good today as I was 27 years ago.

The view across the Eastern Branch of the Elizabeth River from my hotel window today is sure a whole lot better.

Thanks to the efforts of Metro Machine's founding owners and workers, its current employee-owners, its political representatives its subcontractors, its suppliers, its bankers, its lawyers, its accountants, its insurance brokers, its insurance underwriters, its ship brokers and the City of Norfolk; that view is of the new Metro Machine we stand in today.

That new Metro Machine is the newest, most modern, most technically proficient, most secure, most environmentally compliant, most safe, most efficient, and largest private shipyard totally dedicated to the repair and modernization of U.S. Navy ships.

The shipyard is located close enough to downtown Norfolk to be an indispensable source of high paying blue collar jobs unique to heavy industry, but remote enough to, with modern environmental technology, be a good neighbor to white collar workers and visitors essential to downtown.

In the year 2000, when evaluating whether or not to proceed with the new Metro, Metro management faced the same kinds of issues faced by Norfolk leaders in 1970.

Creating a Metro Machine ability to continue in business through the first half of the 21st Century would demand significant facility investments involving very considerable financial risk just like that taken by the City of Norfolk after 1970. The facilities of Metro were bought and paid for by the year 2000 but they were as worn out as downtown Norfolk was in 1970. The Navy was expressing concern for the safety of its ships and personnel in these facilities. Very significant refurbishment of existing drydock, piers, ship services and cranes was judged necessary if these facilities were to continue in long term service.

The Navy amphibious and auxiliary ships that had been the backbone of Metro's workload since 1971 were scheduled for phase-out during the first decade of the 21st Century and were scheduled for replacement by ships too large for Metro Machine's existing Norfolk drydock and piers. Therefore, larger capacity drydock, pier and ship services would be required to continue this traditional Metro Machine work.

The rebuilding of downtown Norfolk in close proximity to Metro plus projected environmental restrictions for air, water and noise mandated significant environmental investments, even though Metro was already the most environmentally advanced shipyard in the World.

All of this faced the Management of Metro Machine as it evaluated the choice between taking this additional risk or risking instead the basic long term employment needs of Metro's employee-owners. This was the very same choice faced by the City of Norfolk after 1970 when it chose to take financial risk to benefit the long term needs of its residents.

You can't tell from the Wilcox Savage 18th floor conference room that the paint being applied to USS Shreveport's flight deck will last years longer because Metro is the only shipyard in the World to invest in 50,000 psi robotic water blasting equipment.

You can't tell from Mayor Fraim's office on the 11th floor of City Hall that paint removed from ships in Metro isn't getting in the Elizabeth River because Metro employs sophisticated collection procedures and equipment that other shipyards refuse to invest in.

You can't tell from Waterside that the 40,000-ton Navy ship entering Speede is being safely handled by four workers instead of the usual 40 because Metro invested in the World's first such equipment.

Like the City of Norfolk, Metro management concluded that long term employee-owner needs for jobs, healthcare, and retirement was no choice at all. The new Metro was conceived based on that decision.

We celebrate the most important aspect of that decision today as we celebrate the installation in Norfolk of Speede Drydock, which was launched and commissioned in Mangalia, Romania.

Getting back to the third Ali – Frazier fight, I remember meeting with Henry Swanner the very next 1975 morning. He impressed me as the most down-to-earth and knowledgeable shipyard executive I had ever encountered. It took me two years, but I finally convinced him to let me join him.

Henry, in all the years before and since that day has been the truest friend and staunchest supporter of everyone who ever worked at Metro Machine. He is the reason each of us is here today. He is here today himself with his wife, Joyce.

Total cost committed for the new Metro Machine facility exceeds 60 million dollars. $20 million dollars of this was with the help of City of Norfolk Enterprise Zone financing through Wachovia Bank.

Producing the profits to service this financing in future years will require the best of all of us. But, we have confronted and overcome much greater challenges as in the past we built and operated this extraordinary enterprise named Metro Machine Corporation.

It has been the joy of my working life to share this experience with you. Thank you for that and this glorious day."

Indeed, that day that Speede Drydock was commissioned and all the days in Norfolk leading up to it had convinced me that only by industries working to make their cities great can they have great cities that are able to help them compete.

My early Norfolk civic participation also convinced me that Girl and Boy Scouting with parental participation does much to make cities great. Our son Rick was nine when I arrived at Metro Machine. He had been a Cub Scout in Mobile so that had to be a family priority in Norfolk.

The first cub scout meeting we attended in Norfolk was a madhouse. I told Janet that, since I couldn't possibly make things worse, I was signing up to be Cub Master Tommy Winder's assistant. Tommy and I turned out to be good friends since our sons were the same age and we both enjoyed having fun with kids.

When Rick came of age, I moved over to the Webelos leader position, which led to Tommy and me doing a lot of camping with the boys. Once we got past forgetting to bring matches to the first campout, we did great. But other packs didn't let us forget about it for months.

Despite the match incident, I progressed to being Assistant Scout Master for the troop and Ski-Co-Ak (Norfolk) District Chairman. Nothing was more fun than our camping trips. While I was pleased to be honored by the Norfolk BSA, my real reward was the time with my Son. It was our best of times. I highly recommend it to all dads. Rick and Vicki are now enrolled in scouting with their own two young boys.

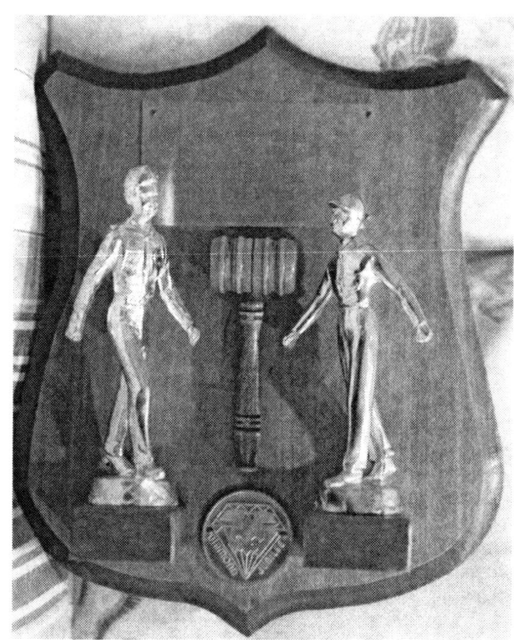

"Outstanding Dedicated Service" SKI-CO-AK, Norfolk, VA BSA 1983

11: Tales of Working with Competitors

By 2010, I had accumulated a unique four-decade history of finding mutually beneficial ways to work with shipyard competitors once the competition was over. This history began with my early leadership of the SNAME Ship Production Committee in 1970. This history led directly to the $165 million sale of the Metro Machine stock owned by the Metro ESOP in 2011.

As Director of Division Planning reporting to the President of Ingalls, I was Ingalls' delegate to the SNAME Ship Production Committee. The other participating major American member shipyards were Newport News Shipbuilding, Bath Iron Works, Todd Shipyards, Bethlehem Steel Shipyards and NASSCO.

The other shipyard delegates selected me as Chairman of the Committee. The committee was considered SNAME's most effective committee, although the industry never became world-competitive because of the very low wage rates prevalent in non-U.S. shipyards.

After I left Ingalls to become Metro Machine CEO, I always remained interested in finding opportunities acceptable to the Navy of working with competitors after contract(s) award to benefit the Navy.

Before arriving in Norfolk, I had worked for 22 years in shipyards in Brooklyn, Staten Island, Groton CT, Quincy MA and Pascagoula, MS. In each case, the shipyard I worked in was the only shipyard in the city and so there was no other local shipyard with which to explore cooperation.

The situation was quite different in Norfolk when I arrived in 1977. There were 14 companies in Norfolk holding U.S. Navy Master Ship Repair contracts and calling themselves repair shipyards. Each had competent managers and workers accomplishing a variety of ship repair tasks. Depending on the particular Navy bidding opportunity, Metro Machine might find itself competing against any or all of them.

There was no cooperation among Norfolk shipyards in 1977. Instead, they competed and performed each bid on a no-holds-barred basis.

The first break in that came in 1982 when I was asked to head up a school to train shipyard workers using Federal funds that had become available for such a program. The funds were intended to train workers for all the shipyards.

I had a vacant old shipyard shop available and suitable for training the recruits. I also had the nerve to ask my fellow shipyard presidents to cooperate with me to make the school a success..

It turned out that I didn't have to do much convincing. Despite the fierce bidding competition among the fourteen shipyard companies, they really saw each other as kindred souls, liked each other, and enjoyed solving problems together.

I was chosen to be President of the newly founded training organization soon named Tidewater Maritime Training Institute. There were never to be any harsh words, but there were plenty of laughs.

The foremost Norfolk repair shipyard was named Norshipco. It had been owned by the Roper family of Norfolk and had been in the drydocking business since the beginning of WW II. Once Old Dominion Drydock was commissioned in June 1982, Norshipco became Metro Machine's primary competitor and it was a tough one indeed.

About a year after Metro Machine's Old Dominion Drydock was commissioned, the drydock Norshipco used to compete with Old Dominion had a tragic fatal accident and was a total loss. The entire east coast shipping and shipyard fraternity expected Metro Machine to use the opening to steal Norshipco's commercial customers. I did not choose to do so.

Instead, I advised Chuck Eure, Norshipco President, that Metro Machine would not approach Norshipco's commercial customers until Norshipco's replacement drydock was in service. In addition, I made all idle capacity of Old Dominion exclusively available to Norshipco to accomplish its previously-contracted commercial ship drydockings. One of these drydock evolutions actually involved temporary relocation of Old Dominion Drydock to the Norshipco shipyard.

This action, combined with the joint operation of the Tidewater Maritime Training Institute, advanced the relationship between Metro Machine and Norshipco. The next opportunity to advance our cooperation came when the Navy made a most unique contract award on two identical Spruance class destroyer upgrades which were to be performed concurrently. Metro Machine was awarded one and Norshipco was awarded the other, obviously to encourage schedule competition between the two rivals.

Much to the surprise of both the Navy and Norshipco, I threw open the gate to Metro Machine and provided Norshipco's managers with access to all non-financial information pertaining to the Metro Machine destroyer production effort. Not to be outdone, Norshipco did the same for Metro Machine's destroyer management team.

It was fulfilling to observe the result. Each company's workforce was convinced it could beat the other, whether the other was watching it perform all its work or not. It was a real squeaker down to the wire for 12 months, with Metro finally completing its destroyer just one day ahead of Norshipco. Metro did this by completing on the original completion date, a performance unmatched on any prior Spruance destroyer overhaul on the East, Gulf or West Coast.

The workers of both companies enjoyed it. Shipyard workers of both companies gained respect for the other. The Navy really liked the result. But, unfortunately, it would be 2010 before the Navy was again able to schedule two nearly identical ship overhauls in two separate shipyards at about the same time.

Meanwhile, in the late 1980s, the Navy suggested the Norfolk repair shipyards cooperate to speak with one voice to the Navy and Congress. The shipyards, led by Chuck Eure and me, responded by telling the Navy they preferred to continue to speak individually to Congress. But, we told the Navy that there were other important issues that could be improved if the Norfolk shipyards worked together with the Navy.

Chuck Eure of Norshipco, Bob Walker of Marine Hydraulics, Bill Thomas of Moon Engineering, Billy Johnson of Colonna's Shipyard and I were to establish an association that would be open to all shipyard companies, whether they owned piers and drydocks or not, including subcontractors.

These same individuals requested me to be the founding President. I felt honored and accepted their request.

The five founders agreed that the best candidates for collective cooperation among Norfolk repair shipyards and the Navy were: worker training, worker safety, environmental compliance, combat systems and contract administration.

The organization was named The South Tidewater Association of Ship Repairers (STASR). I served two years as the founding President of STASR and enjoyed an additional year as President several years later. From its founding, STASR was a model of industry cooperation by trade associations. It changed its name and added a legislative-affairs function in the early 2000s.

RESOLUTION OF APPRECIATION

FROM THE

BOARD OF DIRECTORS

SOUTH TIDEWATER ASSOCIATION OF SHIP REPAIRERS

WHEREAS, the South Tidewater Association of Ship Repairers was formed to maintain high standards in the ship repair industry; and

WHEREAS, Richard A. Goldbach was a founding Director of the Tidewater Maritime Training Institute, and a founding Director of the South Tidewater Association of Ship Repairers; and

WHEREAS, the Board of Directors of the Association elected

RICHARD A. GOLDBACH

to serve as its President from October 1, 1990, to September 30, 1991; and

WHEREAS, under his skillful and diligent leadership, the goals of the Association have been fulfilled, and the status and influence of the Association have been enhanced; and

WHEREAS, he continued close working relations with the officers and staff of the Supervisor of Shipbuilding, Conversion and Repair, Portsmouth, Virginia, by facilitating the on-going work of Association committees working with SupShip personnel; and

WHEREAS, he established a dialogue with the Secretary of Economic Development of the Commonwealth of Virginia, and was instrumental in representatives of that office visiting ship repair yards and other firms of the Association; and

WHEREAS, he led the Association in proactive compliance with federal, state, and local environmental laws and regulations; and

WHEREAS, he furthered environmental knowledge of the members of the Association by presenting speakers on environmental subjects, and by supporting communication with regulatory agencies; and

WHEREAS, he led the Association in establishing a close working relationship with the State Water Control Board, including the appointment of Association members to an ad hoc advisory committee; and

WHEREAS, he supported the Association in efforts to comply with human resources legislation by establishing the Human Resources Committee; and

WHEREAS, he contributed to the improved safety of the shipyard workplace by supporting representation to the OSHA Shipyard Employee Advisory Committee, by co-hosting a regional safety meeting with the Signal Mutual Company, by supporting the Association Safety Awards Program, and by promoting various courses offered to Association companies in shipyard safety and first aid; and

WHEREAS, he worked effectively with the San Diego Ship Repair Association, the Shipbuilders Council of America, and other associations to communicate mutual concerns to federal elected representatives; and

WHEREAS, he recognized the continuing educational needs of the ship repair industry by effectively managing the resources of the Tidewater Maritime Training Institute to provide basic training and continuing education for shipyard trainees, tradesmen, apprentices, supervisors, and managers; and

WHEREAS, under his leadership, the members of the Association improved business and personal relationships among themselves, which strengthened the maritime business community in South Tidewater; and

WHEREAS, Richard A. Goldbach gave of his time, energy, and talents to direct these activities with skillful management;

NOW, THEREFORE, BE IT RESOLVED, that the Board of Directors of the South Tidewater Association of Ship Repairers, in full concert, recognize the contributions of Richard A. Goldbach to the successful operation of the Association and the Tidewater Maritime Training Institute from October 1, 1990, to September 30, 1991; and

BE IT FURTHER RESOLVED, that the Board of Directors extend to him their grateful appreciation for his competent leadership and distinctive service.

I certify that the foregoing resolution was unanimously approved by the Directors of the South Tidewater Association of Ship Repairers, Inc. at its duly called meeting on October 17, 1991.

M. V. Craft, President

STASR Award to Rich fashioned from antique wooden ship hammer used to caulk seams between wood strakes

In 2009, I saw an opportunity for Metro Machine to cooperate with General Dynamics NASSCO in San Diego in a way which could help both shipyards to better serve the Navy. The opportunity was created by the two companies having similar contemporaneous Landing Ship Dock (LSD) multi-ship modernization contracts.

My idea was for Metro Machine and NASSCO to cooperate in a manner similar to the way Metro Machine and Norshipco had cooperated on the 1980s Spruance Destroyer contracts. The Navy had even more to gain on the LSDs than on the Spruance Destroyers because ten ships were involved instead of two.

John Strem, President of Metro Machine, requested Navy permission to discuss with NASSCO's President, openly sharing the same kind of normally-confidential production performance details Metro Machine and Norshipco had shared on the 1980s Spruance destroyers. The Navy agreed. It saw no conflict between Metro Machine and NASSCO, because one was on the East Coast only and the other was on the West Coast only.

John met with the NASSCO President in San Diego. The meeting was cordial. John suggested the reason this concept would be beneficial to NASSCO as well as the Navy was because NASSCO could use the information it got from Metro Machine to earn higher LSD modernization performance fees. The NASSCO President was skeptical that NASSCO could learn enough from the much-smaller Metro

Machine to improve its performance and initially declined John's proposition.

When the Navy heard NASSCO had declined the Metro Machine offer, it suggested NASSCO send a production delegation to audit Metro Machine before it finalized its decision. NASSCO did so and afterwards decided to accept John's offer. Both parties quickly benefited from sharing production details, pleasing the Navy.

After Metro Machine and NASSCO had benefited from sharing LSD modernization production details for about half a year, I received a call from the NASSCO President advising me that the Chairman Designate of General Dynamics, named Phebe Novakovic, had asked to meet with me in Norfolk. The purpose of the meeting was to discuss the possibility of Metro Machine and NASSCO sharing of non-production LSD modernization information, in addition to the production information already being shared.

The meeting with Phebe was cordial and resulted in an agreement for the sharing of financial management information. Phebe stated that this interest in sharing financial management information did not constitute a NASSCO interest in purchasing Metro. I replied that Metro Machine was not for sale.

Nonetheless, after examining Metro Machine's financial information, Phebe requested to meet with me again to discuss a possible price for NASSCO purchasing Metro Machine. I concurred and Phebe gave me the courtesy of traveling to my home in June 2011 for the discussion.

I had examined a number of shipyard sales and concluded from that examination that the price that would be fair to Metro Machine's employee-owners was approximately $165 million. Phebe replied that the accounting ratio commonly known as EBITDA (earnings before the deduction of interest, taxes, depreciation and amortization expenses) would indicate a lesser number.

I replied that, as she knew, I was proud to have worked at the General Dynamics Electric Boat Division when that company, together with the Navy and Lockheed, had saved the World from Soviet nuclear intercontinental missiles, without the term EBITDA yet being invented. I concluded by reasserting that I still believed my asking price was appropriate.

After additional discussions, General Dynamics agreed the price I discussed in my meeting with Phebe was a fair one.

My relationship with Electric Boat had come full-circle during 53 years. The 34 years of Metro Machine success that I had built on top of 10 years of Electric Boat experience was going to be part of Electric Boat when my working days were over. My Metro Machine shipyard creation was to become part of the largest employer of shipwrights in the world.

12: Doctor of Commercial Science

WEBB INSTITUTE CITATION

Richard A. Goldbach

Honorary Degree of Doctor of Commercial Science

Your graduation from Webb Institute of Naval Architecture commenced a career rich with achievement. You were employed in shipyards from 1955 to 2011. These positions included Director of Planning (Estimating, Industrial Engineering, Scheduling, Material Control, Production Control, Facilities, Maintenance) and Submarine Overhaul Director of Ingalls Shipbuilding; General Installation Superintendent (Pipe Dept., Outside Machine Dept., Electrical Dept., Test Dept.)Outfitting Superintendent(Rigging Dept., Carpenter Dept., Launching/Dry Docking Dept., and Cost Engineer of Electric Boat Division; Naval Architect in charge of launching for Bethlehem Staten Island Shipyard.

Metro Machine Corporation, Norfolk, Virginia CEO from 1977 to 2011 and sole trustee for the ESOP Trust that owned 100% of company stock from 1986 until your retirement in 2011. Until its sale to General Dynamics, Metro Machine was the largest privately held shipyard in the United States, measured by sales. Metro Machine exclusively performed repair and alteration of non-nuclear surface ships for the U.S. Navy. Metro Machine was the National Small Business Prime Contractor of the Year in 1981, was the only entity in the U.S. to be honored by the EPA for environmental excellence in 1983, and was awarded the Navy's Aegis Excellence Award in

1993 and 1995.

Amidst a busy and successful professional career, you have also used your energy and wisdom to serve on Boards, have many professional and civic memberships, and hold numerous patents within the United States and abroad.

Webb Institute is proud, and fortunate, to count you among its alumni. The Webb Alumni Association awarded you the William Selkirk Owen award in 1999. If a life's measure is the sum of a series of successful ventures, then surely, Richard Goldbach, yours is triumphant.

Richard A. Goldbach, it is my supreme honor on behalf of Webb Institute to recognize your career of leadership and achievement by conferring upon you the degree of Doctor of Commercial Science, honoris causa.

R. Keith Michel, President *21 June 2014*

13: Tale of Henry's Life and Death

Clyde Bonney is a Metro Machine institution. Every Metro Machine employee knows him. His relationship with the Swanner family goes back to before Metro Machine. He is the longest serving Metro Machine shipwright, the most loyal Metro Machine shipwright, one of the most respected Metro Machine shipwrights, and the most-ornery Metro Machine shipwright. He lost a leg in a Metro Machine forklift accident in 2010 that ended his work but not his Metro Machine associations.

In mid-February 2012, Clyde contacted me with the news that Henry was confined to his bed and was dying. The two of us agreed to travel from Norfolk to Florida together to visit with Henry one more time. It was a joyous occasion with many reminiscences of shared experiences and plenty of laughs. After several hours, Clyde left me alone with Henry.

I told Henry how grateful I was for the trust he had placed in me at a time when no one else would. I told him that the people were wrong who thought he got more out of our relationship than I did because of the money. I told him that, because the job he gave me turned out to be the most fulfilling in shipbuilding, I was the clear winner. I told him that I alone knew what a sacrifice it had been for him to concede to me the opportunity to lead Metro Machine to its success.

I looked into his eyes and told him, for the first time, that I loved him. I hugged him, also for the first time, as he laid there watching me watch him. There we were, two old shipwrights, after 35 years together, still rejoicing in the awesome fulfillment that we had shared.

Afterward, I suggested to Clyde that he and I celebrate the opportunities Henry had given us at Disney World. As I pushed Clyde around the park, he told absolute strangers that he had the CEO of Metro Machine of Norfolk Virginia as his pusher. In the darkness of "It's A Small World", when no one could see him, I could feel Clyde smiling, something he rarely did.

Henry died several days later, knowing all his shipwright friends had shared in the success of his creation, just as he had always wanted.

Henry L. Swanner
February 8, 1919-February 18, 2012

Beloved Husband, Father, Mentor, and Dear Christian Brother Henry L. Swanner of Tidewater, Virginia, beloved husband of Joyce Swanner, died quietly in his sleep at his Weirdsdale, Florida residence on February 17.

Mr. Swanner was best known for investing his entire life savings of ten thousand dollars in the founding of Metro Machine Corporation in 1963 and then building it into the largest independent repair shipyard in the nation. At the time of its sale to General Dynamics Corporation in 2011, Metro Machine was valued at 164 million dollars. Metro Machine earned many honors including being named the National Small Business Prime Contractor of the Year by the SBA, the Leader in Environmental Education by the EPA, and for Aegis Program Excellence by the U.S. Navy.

Metro Machine was a dedicated supporter of the youth of the Berkley Community of Norfolk through the Southside Boys and Girls Club, St. Helena's Elementary School, Campostella Elementary School, Berkley Compostella Early Learning Center and Berkley Senior Center.

When Henry retired from his day-to-day activities as Metro Machine Board Chairman on August 31, 1987, he financed the establishment of the Metro Machine Employee Stock Ownership Plan (ESOP), which acquired all Metro Machine Stock upon his retirement. He continued to serve on the Metro Machine Board of Directors until 1997. The many hundreds of Metro Machine employees whom he befriended, mentored and encouraged during his 34-year association with them, knew Mr. Swanner only as "Henry". Henry's dream was to have his Metro Machine friends be the ultimate financial beneficiaries of their years of work with him. His dream was realized just three months ago when General Dynamics purchased his life's work from the ESOP established for his Metro Machine friends. He will rest in peace.

In addition to his wife Joyce, and his Metro Machine family, Henry Swanner leaves six children: June Munford, James Swanner, Joyce Ruhser, Carol Davis, Katherine Thompson and Ralph Keating.

Part II – Tales of Those Who Most Influenced Me

Janet: The instant we are born we are destined to be a unique, permanent and eternal building block for all members of the chain of life we influence.
Therefore, the instant we are born, we are destined to live forever. Rich

1: Tales of Dad before 1950

Frank P. Goldbach, my Dad, was born in New York City in 1907 even though his mom lived on a farm in Poughkeepsie where she worked as a domestic and her husband worked as a farmhand. His mom, Harriet Goldbach, was determined that all her children would be born in the greatest city in the greatest country in the World.

He was the great grandson of Valentine Goldbach, a German wood carver who immigrated into the U.S. because he could not find work in his own country. Despite his German origins, my Dad would come to help produce the sonars used to sink the German U Boats that sent thousands of patriotic and brave Americans to the bottom of the Atlantic Ocean in World War II.

My dad told of seeing his own dad climbing the farm's windmill to yell directions to New York City to a pilot in an open plane as the plane circled the windmill. He spoke fondly of the farmer's sheepdog for much of his life.

My grandparents moved my dad and his three younger siblings to Kearney, New Jersey, in the early 1920s when my grandfather found work at DuPont Corporation. This placed my dad under the spell of Thomas Edison, who was doing his extraordinary electrical inventing in nearby Menlo Park, New Jersey. It also placed him under the spell of Charlotte, his one and only love!

In 1928, my dad earned a Newark College of Engineering Bachelor of Science Degree in Electrical Engineering in just three years. His graduation coincided with the start of the 1929 Great Depression. Because of living and looking for work through all the years of the Depression, he would be a frugal man for all his life.

He was the first Goldbach in Valentine Goldbach's line to earn a U.S. college degree. Because of his extraordinary mathematical capability, which his sons inherited, he was believed by those sons to be descended from Christian Goldbach (1690 – 1764), a Russian mathematician famous for a conjecture in number theory named after him. Alas, there is no proof or way of acquiring proof, just speculation.

My Dad Frank Picker Goldbach upon receiving a Bachelor of Science Degree in Electrical Engineering from the College of Engineering of Newark, N.J. on June 15, 1928

Dad submitted the following resume to Johns Hopkins Applied Physics Laboratory when discussing employment there in 1951:

"The following resume describes my professional experience for the entire period subsequent to the award of my engineering degree by Newark College of Engineering.in 1928. During this time, I was continuously employed in an engineering capacity in design, development or production work on electronic and electromechanical equipment. To a great extent, my activities were of a technical administrative nature requiring close collab-

oration with management, production and sales at all times. In addition, the diversified line of products that I have been responsible for has permitted me to become thoroughly conversant with all procedures dealing with armed services and commercial contracts, specifications, and requirements. Likewise, I have acquired a wide acquaintance in such fields as represented by the Bureau of Ships (USN), the U.S. Air Force and the motion picture field through direct engineering – customer relationship.

Prior to 1928

At the time of my matriculation with Newark College of Engineering, I was following a cooperative plan in which a part of the engineering course included active participation in industry. Half of my time, during the last two years, was spent with the Westinghouse Electric and Manufacturing Company in Newark, New Jersey where I served as student engineer. During this period, I worked in all departments of this large instrument concern finally winding up in the engineering department.

1928 to 1929

My first position, after graduating from college, was with the Weston Electrical Instrument Corp. of Newark, N.J. I was employed in the Production Control Department as an operation sheet writer. Acting in this capacity, I was in a position where I came in contact with every manufacturing operation in the entire company, thereby gaining considerable experience in machine operations of all types, phenolic molding techniques, plating, finishing, assembly and the like.

1929 to 1933

I worked for two companies during this time, the Jenkins Television Corp and the Deforest Radio Company. They are listed together since the activities were absorbed by the second through a stock merger. My work for both companies was the same and it consisted of the development of mechanical television receivers, direct and indirect pick-up cameras and television receivers, amplifiers and transmitters.

In addition, I installed and operated a number of shows around the country for the purpose of promoting an interest in the new art.

1933 to 1936

I was employed by the Hy Grade Sylvania Corp. of Clifton, N.J. through this period. My duties centered largely about production and production design of electronic and mechanical equipment. For a part of the time, I was in charge of the plant operations which included the manufacture of radio transmitters, radio receivers, automatic vacuum tube manufacturing and testing machinery for affiliated factories and general tools and dies used in the production of "receiver" type vacuum tubes. Since a few types of "transmitting" vacuum tubes were manufactured at the plant where I worked, I also was brought in on some of the problems that arose during production. Considerable experience was gained in manufacturing techniques, production control methods and general factory operations.

1936 to 1940

During this period, I served as Chief Engineer to the Kalorama Laboratories of Irvington, N.J. In this capacity, I directed the activities of an engineering and design force in developing television systems against basic patents controlled by two inventors. It was my duty to prove the practicability of the conceptions for the benefit of an organization of "backers". This work entailed the design and development of television receivers, amplifiers and transmitters, as well as picture producing methods. The developments were aimed directly at large screen picture projection for theatre use. Specific developments included optical devices, light control valves, high speed scanning mechanisms, secrecy transmission systems and some facsimile.

1940 to 1948

As a member of the International Projector Corp. of Bloomfield, N.J, I held the position of Director of Engineering after serving as assistant to this office for several years. My responsibilities in both of these positions were to limit the product design work of the department, operate a production control unit, and coordinate these functions with production, sales and management activities. The general operations of the engineering group included new product design and development, improvement of present product, from the standpoint of manufacturing cost and general customer acceptability, and general study of new ideas.

The regular line of commercial products that were covered during my operations included the following:

1. *Professional 35 mm. motion picture projectors (Simplex Line).*
2. *Professional 16 mm. motion picture projectors.*
3. *Motion picture theatre and sound system (Sound head to loud speakers.)*
4. *Drive In theatre equipment.*

War time and subsequent Armed Services Equipment that was designed and developed included the following:

1. *Survey water depth recorders for the Corps of Engineers, U.S. Army*
2. *Navigational depth recorders and indicators for the U.S. Maritime Commission*
3. *Depth measuring equipment of various types for the U.S. Navy*
4. *Sonar devices for submarine detection for Naval Research Laboratory*
5. *Radio Direction Finders for the U.S. Maritime Commission*
6. *Radar trainers for operators of bombing and gun tracking equipment for the U.S. Air Forces*
7. *Components for the Warden bombsight*

Note that many of the above products were later adapted to commercial use."

....

In 1948, IPC transferred Dad from Bloomfield, N.J. where the family lived in Scotch Plains, to Pleasantville. N.Y. Rob and I were extremely happy with the move because of the Pleasantville sports program offered by "Coach" Kurchek, the Pleasantville music program offered by "Doc" Tellstrom and an interesting newly-discovered species called "girls". But Dad was not happy. After eight years, the management style of IPC no longer measured up to the importance Dad put on showing respect at all times. Dad had learned the importance of respect from his parents and his prior employments. So, he left IPC.

Dad began discussions with Dr. Alvin (Al) Eaton, Director of Johns Hopkins Applied Physics Laboratory (APL) in Silver Spring, Maryland. It was a marriage made in Heaven. Both men were highly respectful of all others at all times. Each had technical and management skills the other did not. Dad went to work for Al in 1951 and worked for him until 1977. The two men inevitably became highly respected best friends and remained best friends until Dad's death in 1991.

But, before Dad and the family left for APL and Silver Spring, an apparently innocuous event took place that would ultimately affect every detail of my subsequent life.

Dad was impressed by a young engineering subordinate in 1949 and one day asked him where he went to college. The young engineer responded, "Webb Institute of Naval Architecture". The young engineer further advised that the "Saturday Evening Post" had just reported Webb was "America's Toughest School".

In those days, almost every family read the same magazines which included "Life", "Colliers", "Reader's Digest" and "The Saturday Evening Post", so this article was really a big deal. The young engineer told Dad all about Webb and Dad was impressed. Dad told the family all about Webb that night at dinner.

Rob and I, aged 14 at the time, were just starting to think about college. We immediately sent off to Webb for a Webb College Catalogue. From the day we received that catalogue in the mail, Webb was our choice and we sent for no other college catalogs.

2: *Tales of Mom*

Frank and Charlotte Goldbach in the 1960s

My Mom's only namesake is her great-granddaughter Charlotte to whom I sent the following letter to in 2010:

"Dear Charlotte,

This is the photo of my Mom and your Great Grandmother, Charlotte Horn Goldbach that I most cherish. It has been passed on down through the family to me. I believe she would want you to be the next keeper of it.

As far as I know, it is the only surviving photo of Charlotte that was taken when her entire adult life was still in front of her.

Standing in the middle next to her is your Great Grandfather's youngest sister Ruth, who considered Charlotte to be her dearest friend and whom Ruth idolized until the day she died. I do not know the friend on the left of Ruth.

Charlotte was born in Jersey City, NJ in December 1907, the first child of immigrants Emma and Frederick Horn. Emma, as a teenager, had heroically emigrated from Basel, Switzerland, rescuing some of her siblings after her own mother, an alcoholic, had deserted them. Frederick was an ex-British soldier.

Frederick had an earlier son, Fred, by his first wife who died in childbirth. John, Margaret, Dorothy, Chris, Matilda (giving me my very own Aunt Tillie) and Helen followed Fred and Charlotte. Charlotte always took much satisfaction in her belief that she was her father's favorite. Helen died in a tragic fire accident in her youth. Chris died of an illness when a young adult.

All the other siblings remained astonishingly close through full lives, although Charlotte did not often visit them. Whenever she did, the give and take between them was a marvel for me, as a child, to behold. The mature Mom I knew would "come alive" with laughter and repartee, a word I never used in those days.

I'm sure growing up entirely in the same tiny two-bedroom house had a lot to do with the closeness between them. Meals were always served in the basement, which opened up to the farmyard, where people, chickens, goats, horses and other animals mixed together.

I believe the special time Charlotte had whenever she got together with her Mom and siblings, especially fun-loving Fred and John, had a lot to do with the special amusement and affection she appeared to feel when your Dad used his imagination to conjure up his own mischief.

This special affection my Mom had for your Dad and the way your Dad returned it must have had a lot to do with you having the honor of being dubbed the only standard bearer for my Mom's given name.

I consider Emma, my Mom's Mom, to be the Matriarch of our family, even though, as a child, I felt overwhelmed and intimidated by her. While Emma was strong willed, she seemed to take in any one that needed help. This sometimes made it impossible for me to understand who was living on her farm when we visited. Sometimes, there were needy people living in her chicken coops.

Frank was first attracted to Charlotte on the streets of Kearney, NJ when a teenager. In his latter days, he told me there was never another woman he was attracted to.

When she was fourteen, Charlotte had to go to work as a telephone operator during the Depression to help feed the Horn family. She also worked for Kreske's Department Store in Newark. According to her, she never opened her pay envelope, just left it unopened on the dining table. Charlotte was never able to return to school because of her family's need for her pay envelope.

Emma took my Father in during the Depression and gave him work because there were no jobs when he graduated from Newark College of Engineering (now part of Rutgers) in 1928 as an electrical engineer. The farm that Emma bought with weekly payments from her change purse over 20 years was, therefore, the first job for a Goldbach college graduate.

Charlotte and Frank married in July 1930.

As the winds of World War II began in Europe, the Depression ironically waned and Frank's vocational selection of electrical engineering turned out to be a very wise one. This vocation led him progressively into pioneering jobs in radio, television, movie projection, radar, sonar and guided missiles. The income from that work permitted Charlotte and Frank to begin a family with Franklin in December 1933 followed by your Grandfather and me in August 1936. It also enabled them to buy a house in Scotch Plains, N.J. in 1939.

One might assume that Charlotte's inability to finish school might have left her at a disadvantage as Frank's career progressively brought him in contact with some of the most advanced technical minds in the nation. This did not happen! Charlotte always more than held her own!

As I was growing up, I always felt the success of Franklin, Robert and I came from Frank, our dad, who was obviously a very successful and highly respected engineer. Eventually though, I came to believe the Goldbach quick-wittedness, which certainly extends through your generation also, came from Charlotte, our Mom and your namesake.

Charlotte played a very aggressive game of Contract Bridge and delighted in outwitting and out bluffing the PhDs, who worked with Frank. She served a year as President of the Scotch Plains, NJ PTA, which she ruled with a very firm hand. She also volunteered at Fort Dix. NJ, helping and giving comfort to the wounded Army soldiers returning from battle in Europe during World War II.

Charlotte remained strong-willed to the end. Frank and "Her Boys", as she called Franklin, Robert and I, were her life. She gave no quarter and lost no arguments. Her Boys were (and are) no different.

I am ever so grateful that, thanks to a most thoughtful decision by your Mom and Dad to have you continue Charlotte Goldbach's name, and thanks to you being you, these important memories return.

With loving thoughts for you and hopes for your future,

(Great) Uncle Rich"

From Charlotte to Rich (in response to above)

"Dear Uncle Rich,

Thank you so much for sending me that letter. I really enjoyed reading it. I want to thank you for sharing something that means so much to you with me. It means so much that you would do that. It is a very important thing to you and by sharing it with me I have learned so much more about my namesake, my great grandma Charlotte, who I only knew for a brief amount of time. While reading the letter I found myself smiling to some parts and to other parts nodding my head understanding more about Charlotte.

The letter was one of the most personal letters that I have read. By reading it, I was able to understand the relationship and friendship that my great grandmother and her husband had. He really seemed to understand her and connected with her and was able to send that advice on to you.

My dad has a copy of a similar letter that your father wrote to my grandfather We have made a copy of your letter to keep with that one so they can be kept together. Along with my dad, my mom has also read your letter.

I would like to tell you that recently I have been given a varsity letter for my sport of choice: field hockey. My number is 16. It is my biggest accomplishment so far in my life and I felt even more accomplished being one of only three other sophomores that were chosen to the 18-player team. I thought that you might like to know.

Thank you again for sending me your letter. Love to you and Aunt Janet.

Love,
Charlotte"

Mom and Dad knew they were going to have their hands full when Robert followed me out of Mom's womb on August 17, 1936 in East Orange, N.J. That made for more than 13 pounds of twins. The U.S. birth rate in 1936 was at an all-time low because of the Depression, but not in the Goldbach family.

When Franklin reached school-age in 1939, Dad's job as Chief Engineer of Kalorama allowed Mom and Dad to fulfill their dream to move from their rented apartment in Maplewood, N.J. to a house they could afford to buy at 30 Park View Drive in Scotch Plains, N.J. All three brothers considered this house to be the house they grew up in and Scotch Plains to be the town they grew up in. Purchase of this house for $5000 enabled Franklin to attend School Number One where "Hank" Bloom, who was to become a close family friend, was principal.

Hank served his country during WW-II. One day, after he came back, he punished the sixth-grade boys for snow fighting by single-handedly taking on the lot of us, including Rob and me, in a one-sided snowball fight. I can still feel his hard-thrown snowballs hit. We surrendered! As we did, we received a lifetime lesson in the perils of overconfidence.

"Bert" Brunner, School Superintendent, lived just three houses away and "Pep" Ehman, Police Chief, lived half-way around the block. It seemed everyone in Scotch Plains knew everyone else. I always felt free but watched-over. Including Rob and me, Bruce Hall, Donald Asper, Herman Fette, Bob Carboy and his brothers, who all lived on the street, there were always enough guys for a pick-up game in something or other, including making firefly lanterns, go fish with cards, snow ball fights, horseshoes, football, softball and belly-whopper sledding. With gas rationing, the streets were our playgrounds.

We walked the one mile to school until the war ended in 1945 and bikes became available. Extra speed was employed when taking the short cut through the Italian neighborhood. I remember being worried one December day when Rob and I were walking to school carrying a Christmas tree we had chopped down in the woods to butter up Miss Laubach. "Pep" Ehman put it in his trunk and carried it to school for us. We thought we had pulled one off but, 70 years later, it seems he must have known we swiped it. As Mom would say, "a guilty conscience needs no accuser."

Charlotte Goldbach was listened to and respected by all the kids and all their parents. When she yelled, Frank, Rob and I came running.

In 1993, after Kristen and Larry walked down the aisle of Duck Church as Man and Wife, Mom took charge. Instead of waiting for the ushers to escort her, she took the arm of Larry's Grandmother Charlotte Etcheverry and the two of them marched down the aisle escorting each other. Everyone smiled.

Charlotte Goldbach and Charlotte Etcheverry after the 1993 wedding vows of Kristen and Larry at Duck Church.

Our deference to Mom lasted to her ending. The three sons in the Goldbach family saw her as being in charge all of her days. Even in her Lewes, Delaware nursing home, she always seemed to be the one giving orders.

Mom's sons were always "her boys." Despite liking the nursing home, she let everyone in it know she had not come to it voluntarily by saying, "My sons dumped me here." She was right, but only based on a technicality. Original arrangements were for her to stay in the nursing home starting at supper and ending at breakfast, with the rest of the time at home with a companion. She soon tired of going back and forth and moved into the nursing home full time.

She believed she had done her job by preparing the three of us to leave the nest without help, which we did. All three of us left home the same week in August 1954; Franklin to marriage. Rob and I to Webb Institute. She moved all our furniture down into the basement by the end of the week. She and Dad spread out in their 1500 square foot house, just in case we had any "smart" ideas about coming back.

The three of us and our wives were near as she fell into a coma when she was 91 in 1998. I messaged her face as she had mine whenever I had a hard time facing the night as a child.

I told her, "Dad is waiting for you".

I was sure she had asked him to be. He loved her so much; he would do anything she asked. He was so smart. If anyone could figure out how to do it, he could. I believe she heard me and believed me.

3: Tales of Naomi

Between 1939 and 1947, all three Goldbach brothers attended School No. 1. Miss Naomi Laubach was Rob's and my favorite School No. 1 teacher.

Much to my delight in 2010, I located a Naomi Laubach Tuxford in California using my newly acquired internet skills. I sent her a letter asking her to confirm she was the same person who had been our teacher.

I was overjoyed to receive her response.

"Dear Richard,

What a welcome and wonderful surprise to hear from you after all these years. I remember you and your brother well, as well as your mother, who commented on the similarity of our names (bach).

Yes, I am the same Miss Laubach, though a bit older (86 years) and I hope somewhat wiser and now answer to the name of Tuxford or Naomi to my friends.

After retirement, we moved to our retirement home at Lake Tahoe, where we enjoyed mountain living before moving to a retirement community in Walnut Creek, CA.

Fortunately, we are still alive enough to be able to enjoy the many activities available to us.

Thank you for your letter and kind words. They made my day – week – year.

Sincerely, Naomi Tuxford"

On August 22, 2010, I sent her a bouquet of flowers and this reply:

"Dear Naomi (taking the liberty of placing myself in the friend category),

Hooray! You are alive and well!

I won't impose on your peaceful life after this. But the only purpose of my first letter was to verify my conclusion that Naomi Tuxford was Naomi Laubach of School Number One. This letter is the one I planned to send to Naomi Laubach if and when I finally found her.

I just celebrated the 50th anniversary of my married life with Janet, my hero and only romantic love, and have just entered the 75th year of my life. These two milestones remind me of how little time I have left to thank those folks who equipped me to navigate through the most dangerous waters of my lifetime.

While I never took the time to understand why, your role in my life has come to mind many times during the sixty-five years that have passed since I was your pupil. Like any college graduate, numerous teachers were involved in my education. But only you remained in my mind over those years, as the teacher that I most hoped to please with my ultimate accomplishments.

I have included a picture of Janet and me at our 50th anniversary banquet celebration and a copy of the write-up from the alumni book for Robert's and my 55th high school reunion. I'm convinced that you played an indispensable role in preparing me to contend with the overwhelming and sometimes terrifying personal challenges that preceded the accomplishments described in that write-up.

I also believe you must have been the standout mentor for many of the kids you taught after Robert and me during your career of forty or so years. I hope you will consider my own thoughts about you, as representative of the affection and respect that I believe almost all of your other pupils must have had for you.

I am certain Robert and I were in the very first class you ever taught, because I remember you mentioning, at the time, that you were only nineteen. What a remarkable age to be given the awesome responsibility for influencing the minds of eight-year old kids, like us.

The School Number One student group, that Robert and I were a part of, had you as a teacher during two grades, as I recall, a partial third grade, and then a full fourth grade.

I remember the kids in our fourth-grade class organizing a surprise party for you. The party was so enjoyable that we did it again, perhaps a month later. I remember you blushing and looking concerned about that second party – with good reason, as it turned out, because the principal thereafter banned all such teacher surprise parties.

Just in case you have ever recalled the incident and wondered about our primary motive for the surprise parties, it really was to return the af-

fection you regularly extended to us. Naturally, we were also aware that ice cream and cake was more fun than schoolwork, but that came second.

I remember running home with Robert after school so we could be there and watch when you and Miss Suron walked by on your own way home to your rooming house, which I think was on Williams Street. One snowy day, we showed our affection by peppering the two of you with snowballs. Apparently, that show of affection crossed the line, because we were chastised by the Principal's office the next day and told never to do it again (which we didn't.) Sincere apologies to you sixty-five years late.

I remember playing softball on days you were the teacher assigned to patrol the playground. I was just an average player but recall trying extra hard whenever you were watching. One of those days, I managed to hit a ball to the fence, which was an astonishing feat for me. You clapped which led to the kids teasing you about me being your favorite and you blushing. I was as close to Heaven that moment as a kid on a playground can get.

Once, when I complained to my father that Mrs. Reynolds was a bossy softball umpire, he complained to you, instead, at the PTA meeting. I was mortified by his error and insisted he correct it. He never did, unquestionably because you were more fun to tease than Mrs. Reynolds.

I have given considerable thought to the reasons why a childhood mentor such as you, during at most 50 weeks, could have played such an important part in influencing my own life's work. It would not have been the knowledge I absorbed, since that knowledge represented quite a small share of the knowledge I ultimately absorbed. It could not have been discipline, since I have no recollection of you needing to take or actually taking disciplinary actions. The only reason I could come up with was this:

"You were the first adult (male or female) to come into my life that conducted herself in a way that made me want to emulate you."

Whether or not my perception was right at the time and whether or not I actually succeeded, I really tried to be like you at a pivotal time of my life.

You mentioned that you are a wiser Naomi now than the one I knew as one of your first students. I'm sure you are right. But the wisdom of the Naomi I encountered at School Number One during World War II was more than sufficient to last the lifetime of this eight-year-old boy as he was just starting to prepare to confront the unknown challenges his life would present.

Whatever happens to you post-86 or to me post-75, nothing can keep that accomplishment from living on. Your long-ago deeds of 1944, when you were barely older than my oldest grandchildren are today, are still alive in me and my offspring as well as the many lives my work and private life influence. Even without the thousand or so other kids who were enlightened by your example during your teaching career, that makes for a pretty good life's work. Congratulations!

With affection, gratitude and fond memories,
Richard Goldbach"

About two years later, on July 19, 2012, I received the following email sent to me from a Pam Kaufhold who was new to me. It said:

"Dear Mr. Goldbach,

My step-mother, Naomi Tuxford, passed away on July 4. While going through her things, I came across your letter to her, written 2 years ago. I don't know if she ever responded, but she kept this letter with her few belongings at her assisted living facility, so I know it had special meaning for her.

She continued to teach after leaving New Jersey, teaching in South America for a few years before coming to CA. where she taught in Burlingame for 20 plus years. It is also where she met my dad. She and my dad retired probably over thirty years ago, and then traveled extensively for many years.

As I said, Naomi passed away July 4. I just wanted you to know your letter was kept by her. As a retired teacher myself, I can wholly appreciate how wonderful it was for her to receive it.

Thank you for your thoughtfulness.
Sincerely, Pam Kaufhold"

I sent the following response to Pam the same day:

"Dear Pam,

Your thoughtful message was very important to me, more important than you could possibly have realized.

My twin Robert and I were among Naomi's very first students, as she was only nineteen when she started teaching our class during WW II at Scotch Plains, NJ School No. 1. Our class had her first for a partial third grade, then again during all of fourth grade.

All our classmates felt very unique love and caring from Miss Laubach, which is the name by which we knew her. All of us returned that special affection, along with the enormous respect one can only feel for someone you know respects you.

I carried my affection for, respect for and gratitude towards Miss Laubach through the following 66 years of my life. My thoughts very frequently returned to her and the significant role I believed she had played in my life's success. I am convinced I chose my wife, Janet, because she made me feel the same way Miss Laubach had.

It was extremely frustrating over all of those years to be convinced that Miss Laubach would never learn of my feelings.

Then, through the miracle of the internet, I found her, married to your Dad, having taught in California. I was finally able to communicate to convey to her some idea of the effect I felt she had on my life. I did get one short response from her but I couldn't tell from that response whether she fully sensed her importance to my life.

Your much-appreciated message indicates that she did and that her importance to me was important to her.

Being convinced of that, I will always feel I was with her when she died. What more beautiful ending could I possibly ask for?

With most sincere gratitude,
Richard Goldbach"

The third grade Rich that remembers Naomi.

I – 4: Tales of Janet before 1960

Janet and Gerri Larson in Colon, Michigan

Janet with magic icon Harlan Tarbell at Abbotts in Colon, MI

Janet and Johnnie Platt at Abbotts Magic Get-Together in Colon, MI

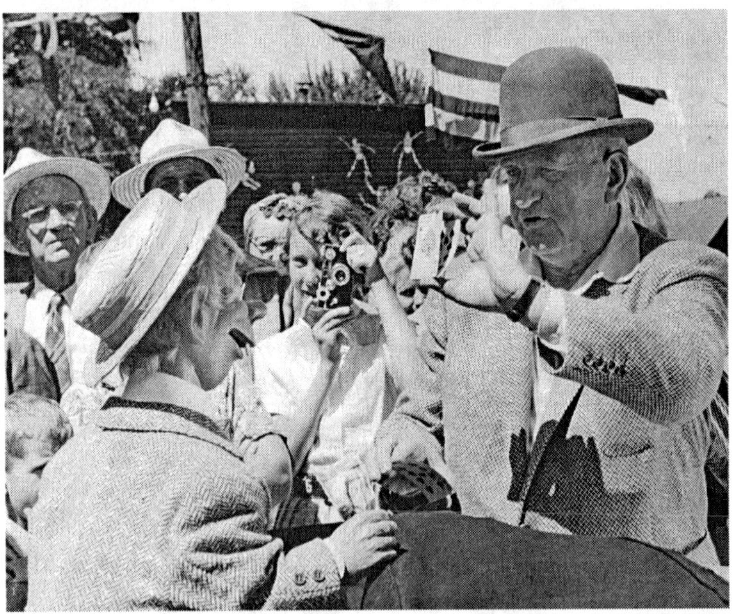

Janet meeting Mortimer Snurd at Abbotts get-together in Colon, MI

Janet, Ruth and Frank on Hicks Street

"Rich-

I believe that we are magic, that all things are possible, that life is precious, that peace is reasonable, that laughter is special, that blessings are divine, that love is grand and that you are the best thing that's ever happened to me. (by I Believe)

I love you, Janet"

Janet Clinton (Janet) was born and raised on Brooklyn Heights which is one square mile located in Brooklyn, New York. She was the daughter of Frank and Ruth Clinton. Working as a magic entertainer, Frank Clinton was credited with being one of the busiest of New York's professional performers. He was known as a fine showman with a light friendly style who was in constant demand.

Frank taught Janet some magical effects so she might audition for a television Special. Janet was chosen from the audition, but in the early years, it was required that no child under the age of eight could be televised and Janet was still only seven years old. The Special was postponed for several months until Janet turned eight. Chosen, Janet caught the "magic bug" and became the darling of the U.S. magic fraternity when she was eight, as she practiced the art of magic entertainment in Frank's style. To members of that fraternity, she was just "Janet" and that was how she was billed whenever she performed for them.

Invited to be a contestant on all of the television contests, she walked away the winner of each one, including one in which she outperformed thirty-eight other weekly winners, all of whom were adults. Soon she was appearing on all the New York stations and at the age of ten was offered her own weekly show. To Janet's dismay, her mother turned down the offer saying "No! She has too much homework to do." That offer was, however, the beginning of many other television shows, primarily in New York, Michigan, Illinois, Massachusetts, Alabama, Mississippi, and Virginia.

A large portrait of ten-year-old Janet by the famous theatrical photographer, Boris Bakchi, was prominently hung in the window of the famous Theatrical Pharmacy in Times Square in 1948. It remained in that same place of honor for over 30 years.

The modest apartment Janet lived in with her parents on 195 Hicks Street was a revolving door of celebrities for the emerging protégé.

Janet couldn't believe her parents would let Roy Rogers come for a light after-the-show meal and leave in the middle of the night without waking her. But, she was awake whenever the famous magician Harry Blackstone Sr. came by. There is a very famous magic fraternity picture of Harry grabbing a broom and impulsively sweeping up rice Janet had dropped while carrying on props before her act.

Janet was also awake whenever Walter Gibson, the creator of the famous radio character, Lamont Cranston, came to visit. Lamont Cranston would turn himself into "the Shadow" whenever required to defend justice on Saturday night radio in the 1940s. My entire family and almost every other family in town everywhere would gather around the radio whenever "the Shadow" came on. How exciting it was for me to meet Walter Gibson in the flesh decades later and find out my wife had actually known my favorite "crime-fighter".

Janet began winning contests at magic conventions where she was also one of the favorite performers on evening headline shows. Her fellow performers looked forward to watching her from year to year as she "grew up" in front of them as a professional performer. Stories about Janet's success as a "girl magician" were published in Cosmopolitan, American Girl, Junior Scholastic, and other national magazines.

One of Janet's performances was at the renowned Illustrators Club in New York. In the audience was the famous illustrator, Jimmy "the Hat" Hatlow. Sure enough, one of "the Hat's" better known comic characters, "Little Iodine," showed up on the cover of her next comic book mimicking one of Janet's tricks just as he had told Janet she would. However, since Little Iodine was prankish, scheming and always at odds with her parents, nobody mistook her for the refined and lovely Janet.

Janet stayed busy as a performer during the last nine years she attended the renowned Packer Collegiate Institute in New York. It took "real magic" to balance the mountains of homework, for which Packer was famous, with the demands of her stage and TV performances. After graduating from Packer with honors, Janet attended Tufts University in Boston, from which she graduated magna cum laude.

In 1958, Janet became the first female invited to perform magic on the stage of the Magic Circle of London, the most prestigious gathering of magicians in the world. She was awarded their bannerette, a most coveted honor. Decades would pass before other women were invited to perform on that same stage.

5: Tales of William

September 30, 1999
Acceptance of W. Selkirk Owen Award
by Richard A. Goldbach

The following was read by Janet because of Rich's Laryngitis

"There are a very few of life's honors that inspire universal respect, just by their mention. Winning the Congressional Medal of Honor is one.

Progressing to Eagle Scout is another.

What is there in the Marine Field other than gaining admittance to and graduating from Webb Institute?

Today and every day, I have to pinch myself so I can realize anew that I really am one of those graduates; that I really am living the fulfilled life that honor has supplied.

For me as with most of you; my career, my marriage, my family, my friends and my civic life have all flowed directly from attending Webb.

I hope that each of you feels the same sense of wonder to be part of William Webb's astonishing contributions to the marine industry, the lives of those who attended his institution, the lives touched by those lives and the continuum.

Thanks to Ed Dunbough, I have been able to visit and revisit my roots in the lives of William Webb and our other benefactors.

Preparing for tonight, I revisited these roots again asking the questions:

- *How did I get here?*
- *Who was responsible?*
- *What character traits led them to do what they did?*
- *What character traits enabled them to do what they did?*

For all of us, the answers start in 1775 when Henry Eckford was born in Scotland, emigrated to Canada, apprenticed there as a shipwright, moved to New York City to start his own shipyard and built a reputation as a first-class shipbuilder by the age of 30; hiring William Webb's grandfather Wilse along the way.

Henry Eckford showed what he was made of when the going got tough in 1807 when Thomas Jefferson banned all trade with belligerents France, England, Germany and Russia during the Napoleonic Wars putting all New York shipyards out of business.

Fortunately for all of us, he wasn't a "woe is me" type so he packed up and headed for Lake Ontario where there was work - building the brig Oneida to protect us from a northern invasion by the Brits.

Two years later when Jefferson lifted the ban, Henry Eckford used the wad of money he had made on Lake Ontario to return to New York, buy out his partner, move his shipyard to a new location and put his prior employees, including Wilse Webb, back to work.

Henry Eckford had no way of foreseeing the ultimate enormity of the impact of his actions on Isaac Webb, William Webb, all of us and the nation.

The second major character in our legacy entered our lives at this juncture, Wilse's son Isaac aged 15.

Much is revealed about both these major characters by Ed Dunbaugh's report of their first meeting.

Isaac showed the persistence which would, time and again, prove vital to maintaining the chain of events leading to our presence here tonight.

Isaac wouldn't stop badgering Wilse until Wilse reluctantly approached Henry Eckford to ask him to meet with Isaac to listen to Isaac's plea to learn shipbuilding.

Henry Eckford agreed to the meeting which was a long meeting. At the end of the meeting, decisions and commitments were made. In one year, Isaac would come to work and live with Henry Eckford for five years to learn everything about both shipbuilding and manhood, that Henry Eckford could convey. This five years of mentoring would ultimately extend to a lifetime.

We weren't born yet, of course, nor were our parents, grandparents, great grandparents or great great grandparents. But two decisive men of honor and vision, one thirty-four and one fifteen (and previously unknown) decided that day not only what they would do with their lives but also what all of us would do with ours. Does that stagger your imagination the way it does mine? or make you wonder how seemingly self-involved decisions of our own might impact others years in the future?

Just three years later, Henry Eckford got another chance to show what he does when the going gets tough. The Brits blockaded our harbors in the war of 1812 shutting all the shipyards including Eckford's - opportunity lost.

The same war threatened the northern New York Great Lakes border. Opportunity created since this northern threat demanded a new Great Lakes fleet. Henry Eckford packed up in 24 hours and headed north again. This time he took 40 workers and Isaac with him.

The Great Lakes fleet prevented a British invasion making its own contribution to our history. Henry Eckford then came home and restarted his New York shipyard.

Henry Eckford's unerring ability to persevere and decisively do the right thing served his country while keeping his and Isaac's aspirations alive and although he had no concept of our eventual existence, keeping all of our dreams alive at the same time. Meanwhile, Isaac was watching and learning.

Another crossroad was reached soon after the war.

Isaac's apprenticeship ended.

Henry Eckford, with vision and unselfishness, explained to Isaac his three options.

- *Stay with Eckford*
- *Leave for a better opportunity at another shipyard*
- *Open his own shipyard with continuing support from Eckford.*

Isaac made the most courageous choice which was to open his own yard. His first job was a subcontract from Eckford. While his own courage, self-confidence and ambition drove Issac's choice, we are the ultimate beneficiaries since this is the only choice which could have kept our dreams alive.

Our day has once again been saved, first by Henry Eckford's vision, ability to judge a man's worth, and desire to help worthy others, secondarily by Isaac's ambition, self-confidence, and courage.

You might ask why I choose to bring up Henry Eckford's vision at this juncture so I'll explain my reasons which admittedly are speculative.

Henry Eckford had plenty of evidence by this time of the unforeseeable cycles that his business was subject to. One way of coping with those cycles was to have competent, trustworthy subcontractors who were loyal to him to absorb expansion above the normal business demand so that absorbing the down cycles was largely their responsibility, not his. Who better than apprentices who had lived with him, absorbed character traits important to him, learned details of the business from him, were grateful and loyal to him and whom he had come to know intimately and trust.

Ed Dunbough's history of our three benefactors describes numerous incidents where just such subcontracting with companies owned by Isaac Webb and other contemporary graduate apprentices, in fact, took place.

His apprenticeship over, Isaac was free to marry and did so, marrying Phoebe. One year later, Phoebe gave birth to William Henry Webb.

The 24 years of shipyard operations by Henry Eckford and Isaac following William Webb's birth and the 32 years of shipyard operations by William Webb which followed that as described by Ed Dunbough, provide fascinating reading. Upon rereading it or reading it for the first time, I guarantee that each of you will find parts of your own career and character displaced by over 100 years.

If the fateful meeting between Henry Eckford and the 15 year old Isaac was really the launch of the Webb Institute starship, as I believe, and the decision by Isaac, after completing his apprenticeship to establish his own enterprise was the first and most important course adjustment, then this 56 years provided most of the information gathering and resource collection which would permit the Webb starship to reach its 19th century destination, the founding of Webb Institute and the Society of Naval Architects and Marine Engineers.

This part of the voyage is full of immense challenges encountered and overcome. It is full of extraordinary opportunities encountered and exploited. It is full of companionship, interdependence, loyalty, trust and respect between exceptional men which is the stuff of life itself. It is full of hard work, bitter disappointment, courage, exhilaration, attention to detail, decisiveness, adaptation, vision and honor. It is full of choices not made because they were cowardly or dishonorable, any one of which would have led all of us someplace except here.

It is full of courageous choices, and enormous obstacles overcome, every one essential to our presence here, which were made because they were right and honorable. It is full of lessons for an evolving William Henry Webb, the pilot during the last 60 years of the journey. It is full of lessons for us.

These evolving lessons and compassion for fellow travelers were absorbed by William Webb, as he steered the Webb starship through and around storms to varied and numerous opportunity way stations, where he restocked and refueled until he discovered and landed at his ultimate destination. He there soundly planted these lessons for the benefit of those who would pass through this destination to further destinations of their own.

There is no challenge that any of us has encountered, or will encounter, that is any greater than those already encountered on this voyage by each of our three benefactors.

Neither have we nor will we encounter more challenges than they did.

Neither have we encountered, nor will we encounter, fewer opportunities than they encountered and exploited.

The oceans remain just as vast as they were. They still dominate every aspect of human existence as they have for the past 10,000 years.

Twentieth century Trade between the inhabitants of this planet was many times the trade during the nineteenth century when our benefactors' portion of our voyage took place. Trade during the 21th century, will explode, providing even greater challenges and opportunities.

Challenges to the planet's ability to conduct that trade will also explode, as trade explodes and technology advances. These challenges must, and will be, met. This ability to trade by sea must and will be defended.

Who will overcome these challenges? Who will exploit these opportunities?

I believe with all my heart that our voyage is the same voyage launched by Henry Eckford and Isaac Webb, commanded first in the 19th century by Henry, Isaac and William Webb, next commanded through the twentieth century by hundreds of Webb followers including William Selkirk Owen armed with the lessons instilled by those benefactors who I believe were the greatest of our Webb Institute teachers.

What a joy it is for me to be on that voyage. What an honor it is to be one of you, the elite group that makes up the crew currently responsible for the voyage. How I hope that our 21st century followers will view our ultimate stewardship of this leg of the journey, the way I view the stewardship of our predecessors.

I believe in us and the legacies of human values and obligations that are ours, because of being graduates of Webb.

I believe that by dedicating our careers to living by these values and fulfilling our obligations to our benefactors at every opportunity, one or more of us will inevitably make choices and accomplish deeds that have the potential to bring enormous benefit to our industry and those engaged in it, hundreds of years from now. And like Henry Eckford, Isaac Webb and William Webb, those chosen for this role will never, in their lifetimes, have any concept of the ultimate impact or identity of those pivotal decisions or deeds. Fulfillment will come from knowing each day has been lived by human values passionately believed in, those ingrained in us by our three benefactors.

How grateful I am for the opportunity the special recognition of the W. Selkirk Owen award has provided, to stand before you, and express these beliefs.

Thank you.
Richard Goldbach"

Henry Eckford

William Webb

6: Tales of Dad after 1950

In July 1960, Dad shared with me what he had learned about living with and loving a wife during his then thirty years of marriage:

"Dear Rich,

It was good to hear from you again the other night and to find you were reporting progress on the renovation work. As I told you, we had already received a letter from Janet telling us of your new address and from the way she spoke, it seems as though she was very happy with the choice you made. I hope you continue to have the very good luck in obtaining the pleasant housing arrangements you have had up till now.

Down here, we have had company all week. Carol's mother stayed with us from Sunday until Tuesday morning and from Tuesday evening through tomorrow, we have had Mrs. Barnett and daughter Merrie. They drove down from Pine Plains, NY in the latter's Austin Healy and as usual managed to get lost. Fortunately, I only had to drive to White Oak to recover them. I almost was late to work this morning because of the AH. Since they were asleep when I left and their car had mine blocked, I had to back it out. However, it took me about 10 minutes to figure out that darned reverse. I still don't know what I did.

Well, son, I guess this will be my last letter to you as a single Man so, I think I'll take a final advantage of a father's privilege and try to offer a few words of what, at least, I think is good advice. Don't feel too bad – your two brothers had to go through it too.

First of all, let me say once more how happy Mother and I are in your choice of Janet as your wife. Her graciousness, humor, and bright as well as practical outlook on life has endeared her to both of us. Her parents, who are tops in our book, have done a wonderful job. You have a big responsibility ahead – keep her that way, for yourself primarily, but for the rest of us as well.

I am sure by now you have discovered that women are different from men (I really don't mean this to be facetious). Their mental processes and general approach to things in our everyday life are not always the same as ours and, therefore, even if you have strong feelings in certain matters, learn to understand and respect your wife's reasoning behind what she says or does with respect to them. I think you'll find more often than not she may be right, regardless of the process or logic she used in arriving at them.

Above all else treat her with the respect due any equal partner in any relationship. Respect her privacy when she desires it, avoid vulgarity like a plague, do everything in your power to prevent her any humiliation because of a thoughtless act on your part. Naturally, you will see that it does not come from anyone else.

Never quarrel for the fun of quarreling. With two persons living as close together as a man and wife there are bound to be enough quarrels that just can't seem to be avoided. Just remember though, to try to see both sides, hard as it may seem, and whatever you do, never go to sleep until it is settled – even though it means giving in a little. As an engineer, you know you have to a put a little more into things than you expect to get out – apply this to your personal relationships and I will guarantee that everything will work out well.

Continue the personal touches you have learned during your courtship. Strange as it seems, a few flowers or a small gift, personally selected by yourself, means more than the most expensive fur coat if the assistance of others is required for its purchase.

On the practical side, make your wife a real partner. Don't do like so many men and keep your finances a secret. I recommend making her your treasurer. Then she knows exactly how things stand in regard to spending. Sure, in the beginning she'll make mistakes but don't we all. In the long run, however, I think you'll find you're better off. There is another good reason to let her handle the finances. In the event that something happens, she will be far more capable of taking care of herself.

Well, that's the end of my preaching for good – please forgive my long windedness. I really don't think it was necessary because I have the utmost confidence in your inherent capability of doing the right things at the right time. So, I'll leave this off with one big wish - "may Janet's and your life be as happy and fruitful as that of Mother's and mine". I couldn't possibly wish you better.

Love,
Dad

See you next weekend."

Dad's work experience after 1950 was best summarized in the 1991 obituary prepared for Dad by his best friend Alvin R. Eaton, Senior Fellow and Director of Special Programs for the Johns Hopkins University Applied Physics Laboratory, Laurel, Maryland:

"Born in New York, N.Y., Mr. Goldbach joined the Applied Physics Laboratory in 1951 after a distinguished career of more than 20 years in industry, having served as Plant Manager, Chief Engineer and Director of Engineering for major organizations involved in the early development of television, motion picture and underwater sound equipment.

At the Applied Physics Laboratory, he became a specialist in weapon system design, and integration, program planning and management, and technical director of contractor activities. He made significant contributions to the design and manufacture of the first U.S. Navy missiles to be widely deployed.

APL Retirement Gift to Frank P. Goldbach

He invented and led the development of missile design requirements documentation and interface control methods that became the systems-engineering standard for a wide range of programs, and received many commendations for his innovative efforts. In connection with the air war over Vietnam, he was responsible for the planning of a test range designed to de-

termine the effectiveness of aircraft tactics and countermeasures techniques, and was recognized as a member of a team that dramatically improved survivability for U.S. aircraft.

APL Retirement Cartoon to Frank P. Goldbach

Mr. Goldbach retired from the Applied Physics Laboratory in December 1975, and resided in Silver Spring, Maryland, prior to moving to Delaware in 1990. Survivors include Charlotte, his loving wife of 60 years, three admiring sons including Franklin Guy Goldbach, Richard Albert Goldbach and Robert Douglas Goldbach and five grandchildren.

Dad portrait in the early 1980s. Painted by Janet Goldbach.

Rear Admiral Wayne Meyer best described the way the Navy viewed Dad's work on behalf of his country when My Dad retired from Johns Hopkins Applied Physics Laboratory in 1975:

DEPARTMENT OF THE NAVY
NAVAL SEA SYSTEMS COMMAND
WASHINGTON, D.C. 20362

IN REPLY REFER TO

23 December 1975

Mr. Frank P. Goldbach
Fleet Systems Department
Applied Physics Laboratory
The Johns Hopkins University
Laurel, Maryland

Dear Frank,

On the occasion of your retirement from the Applied Physics Laboratory, I would like to express the appreciation of the Navy Department for your many years of dedicated service to the needs of the operating fleet.

As an organization, APL is regarded as one of the Navy's most productive technical resources. Two generations of Navy officers and civilian employees have come to expect outstanding support from the scientists, engineers, technicians and other staff members of this fine institution.

Over the years, in the course of many visits to the Laboratory, we have come to know you as one of the Laboratory's quiet leaders in organizing, directing, and supervising complex technical activities. We are particularly grateful for your outstanding efforts in the development of systems integration techniques. The P&CR document concept which you conceived and refined was a foundation for orderly development of many of our most important weapon systems. In similar fashion, the Correlation Drawing approach to missile round integration became an ordnance engineering fundamental, contributing immeasurably to our current arsenal of reliable and capable fleet missiles.

I should also note your role in helping to create the Joint APL/SMS Project Management Study Group Report in 1965, known yet as "the gray book". Through that effort, the Navy and APL not only clarified their operating relationships in the complex business of combat systems RDT&E, but also brought improved order and efficiency to scores of other organizational functions related to Surface Missile Systems. I believe it was a major contribution to the Navy's SMS program.

Be assured that your excellent work has been widely appreciated by the naval ordnance community. Your fine professional touch will be missed. We wish you good health and many enjoyable years of well-earned retirement.

Good sailing!

Very sincerely,

WE Meyer
RAdm US Navy

Navy letter to Frank P. Goldbach upon his Retirement

Part III - Tales of Janet after 1960

1: Tales of Courting Janet

Against all odds, I met a most perfect example of womanhood and humanity on a blind date. Miracle of miracles, despite my insensitivity, I realized it had happened. It was obvious that I was a clod who was not even remotely qualified to compete for her affections. What saved me was that I was too smitten to realize that, so off I went to the chase.

She turned out to be just as cleverly elusive during the hunt as she was perfect. She surely made it fun to chase her.

The wisdom that finally wound up working for me four years later was about tunnels and how we enter them not knowing where they come out. That sure is what happened to us. But, wherever we came out each time, there Janet was alongside me paddling as hard as she could.

It has taken me quite a while to get the hang of always remembering to please the other person in my marriage. We're now at 57 years and counting and I still have a way to go. Janet caught on to it at the altar – no surprise.

When Janet and I found a second floor three room apartment in Noank, CT, she immediately became the perfect homemaker. When she was recruited by the local school principal, she became the most perfect teacher of the worst first grade class to ever go through the Groton School System. When she and I stayed home one Snow Day, she gave birth to Kristen and became a perfect Mom. When it was time to do it again, she procured a basal thermometer and produced Ricky, right on schedule. When we moved to Mobile, Alabama, she showed me what a perfect Mom squared looked like.

2: Tales of Janet Performing Magic after 1960

In 1965, it was time for Janet to resume entertaining the audiences that hadn't seen her since she left for Tufts University in August 1956.

As a result of her fame as a youthful magical entertainer, the world of entertainment always knew Janet, the lovely child, as Janet Clinton. After Janet graduated from Packer, made her society debut, emerged from Tufts as a beautiful adult woman, married an admiring me in 1960, gave birth to Kristen in 1961, and moved to the Boston area; Janet and I both believed it would be unthinkable for Janet Clinton to be lost to the World.

So, after creating theatrical personas for both children and adults, Janet retained her maiden name, "Janet Clinton" as her stage name, and became the most popular magician in town. Costumed in a highly feminine version of the traditional top hat and tails, she presented stage magic and illusions for grown-up audiences, performed on stage, on television, at company sales meetings, clubs, parties and picnics.

Janet enjoyed stepping out on the stage and seeing an audience of strangers, each person arriving with his or her own worries, thoughts and problems; gradually become one harmonious group. Smiling and laughing, they would temporarily forget the problems of the day as they enjoyed being brought together by the fun of Janet's magic.

Janet in 1966

Janet most enjoyed entertaining children. She developed her own character role as "Pixie." Wearing a high conical hat and costumed to portray a mischievous magical sprite, who might have stepped out of the pages of a children's story book, she drew her young audiences actively into magic fun as they helped Janet make it all happen.

Whether Janet was performing as a glamorous refined female or as Pixie; the extraordinary gentle manner of Frank Clinton always came through to her audiences. Keeping in character, Janet's highly successful approach to humor was always original and always all her own, especially her puns. She continually amazed her family members and friends with her ability to pun by gently pouncing on a word just as the pun recipient finished saying it.

Some of Janet's most rewarding personal experiences occurred when she was using magic to entertain children in hospitals. She often told of a little boy, seriously burned, in an accident, who was wheeled in to see one of her shows. His head and body were encased in a protective plaster cast. He sat silently, withdrawn, hardly watching at first. Then, all of a sudden, he began to laugh and call out, joining in the fun. At the end of Janet's performance, the adults and children who had been watching were wheeled back to their rooms.

But this little fellow remained, chatting happily and excitedly as Janet packed up her show. A small item Janet had performed was when she had taken a sheet of newspaper, folded it into a cone shape and poured a full pitcher of milk into that cone. Stepping carefully toward the youngsters, she had snapped the newspaper cone open and to the children's delight, the milk was gone. Laughs came soon again as Janet showed the other side of the paper with a cartoon cat complete with a drop of milk. "I see where it went, my kitty cat drank it!"

This young boy asked Janet if he could have the newspaper she had used when making the full pitcher of milk mysteriously disappear. He said he never wanted the milk the nurses brought him to drink, so he would tape the newspaper on the wall next to his bed and use it to make any milk the nurses bring him disappear. Janet gave him the special newspaper, something she had never done before.

Janet in 1966

After the staff took the young lad back into his room, three of the nurses approached Janet as she was preparing to leave. With much emotion, they told Janet that the little fellow had been in the hospital eleven days. He had refused to utter a word to anyone. They felt it was like a miracle, that had occurred right in front of them. They said that "real magic" had taken place.

Other such "miracles" seem to have occurred as children felt the caring Janet projected as she entertained them. One of Janet's practices which contributed to their enjoyment was her careful composing of each performance to precisely match both the circumstances and the ages of each audience. The audience for one show was in a large school in which the children had mental, physical, or both mental and physical deficiencies.

Janet's more traditional children shows encouraged audience members to become intertwined with the entertainment, becoming excited, calling out, reaching out to her and often a few being invited, to join her on-stage to be "magician's assistants." However, this particular performance was specially designed to let the young folks participate verbally from their seats and wheelchairs.

Following her performance a woman came backstage as Janet was packing up. She said she had been standing next to a woman who had tears running down her cheeks while holding her five-year-old son throughout the performance. Concerned, she had asked the woman if there was any way she could assist her.

She wanted Janet to know what the woman had said in response. It was "My son has never uttered a sound in his entire life. He got so excited during the show that he yelled out three words making an entire sentence." If not a miracle, this certainly showed the awesome power of Janet's caring.

Janet often used her active and inquisitive mind to respond to creative challenges of working out practical methods to respond to unusual requests. A sales executive for a large corporation made one of these . Hired by a national food company to entertain its top salesmen meeting at a swanky resort hotel, Janet was given a list of requested "magic" the company had dreamed up to inspire sales enthusiasm for a new line of soy substitutes for beef, chicken and ham.

Taking for granted that a magician should be able to do anything, the company had four main requirements for the show. Janet was asked to magically make soybeans appear, turn the soybeans into live cows, chickens, and pigs and then transform those into money. On top of this, she was asked to invite on stage a veteran employee, change him to look the way he looked when he first entered the company and finally change him back to his present self.

"I fashioned the show around those requests and added other related ideas," Janet said. "But there was one exception. I didn't produce live cows or pigs-only chicks. I still wonder what the hotel personnel would have done if I had arrived there with cows and pigs in tow through the lobby"

Janet's father, Frank, was President of the Parent Assembly of the Society of American Magicians (SAM) in New York City, where he knew Harry Houdini. Janet joined her father as a member of the SAM Parent Assembly in 1966. Active in half a dozen other societies of magicians, clowns and professional entertainers, Janet was secretary of the Boston Ring of the International Brotherhood of Magicians. She was slated to become the ring's vice-president in 1968 when I took a shipyard position in Mississippi and Janet had to transition to entertaining in Mobile, which led to her being named "The South's Leading Lady Magician." After having to move again, this time to Norfolk, Virginia in 1977 to enable me to take the CEO position of Metro Machine, Janet continued her role as "The South's Leading Lady Magician". She also served as President of the Norfolk Ring of the International Brotherhood of Magicians and was named that Ring's "Stage Magician of the Year."

After performing in New York and Boston for twenty years, Janet was faced with reestablishing herself as an entertainer in the South where many of the people she met were surprised to discover there was a woman who presented magic shows. It didn't take long before Janet was averaging five or six shows a week, performances of all kinds as before, but specializing in children's entertaining. During the nine years Janet performed in Mobile and twelve years in Norfolk VA, Janet performed hundreds of shows annually. "Janet Clinton as Pixie" became so well known that wherever she went youngsters would call out, "Hi

Pixie!"

Their recognition continually pleased and surprised Janet because she thought she looked and acted very different out of costume as she pushed a grocery cart or filled a car at the gas station.

While more and more business and government folks in Norfolk came to know me as Metro Machine grew, I always remained invisible to kids and their moms when I was with Janet. Lamont Cranston, "The Shadow", had nothing on me. Janet clouded the minds of adoring kids much better than "the Shadow" ever could.

Always one of the friendliest of people, Janet used her magic performing as a "friend-maker." It helped her to meet many "delightful and warm people, magicians and lay folk alike". Janet was convinced that magic performing was an "unbelievable personality expander and booster both for herself and for her children."

Excepting for a few dire emergencies, I never performed as her assistant. However, I always encouraged and supported Janet as I packed and unpacked her station wagon and stood in the wings enjoying her shows, smiling, laughing and always feeling proud of her. I did strive to imitate Janet's use of humor as I tried to use my own quite different style of humor to inspire my employee-owners .

When Kristen was born, doctors said she might never be able to speak, but Kristen had excellent medical care and spoke clearly in her own magic shows while performing magic at an even younger age than Janet, when she first started. When Kristen was only seven, she won first place in the junior contest at a national convention of the Society of American Magicians. She won again at the age of nine, and a third time when she was eleven. When a teenager, she gave shows at libraries, schools and churches.

Both Janet and Kristen had quiet off-stage personalities. But in costume, with an audience out front and a show that was fun to perform, a new world always opened up for both of them. When Janet and our family moved to Norfolk, Virginia in 1977, the garage and another room in the house were turned into magic rooms, so Janet and her father could continue their magical lives.

Janet frequently said, "I am really grateful to magic for being the sort of a profession which helped me to express my personality in a way that entertained and which also added a new dimension to the lives of all our family members. It provided confidence and a feeling of being special to shy children like Kristen while also being a wonderful outlet for children like our son Rick, who was more extraverted. Magic has contributed to all our lives in different ways."

.Janet's magic performing parents, Ruth and Frank, came to live with Janet, Kristen, Rick and me when they retired in 1971. Frank continued to use his love of magic by teaching students and lovers of magic for the rest of his active days. For five years, Frank also played the most beloved Santa in Mobile, as he brought his special bells, luxurious beard, book of, "Who's Been Good?" and personal warmth while finding candies and small trinkets behind the ears of a child. Playing Rudolf for Frank as we drove to the next home on the list, I had the best seat in the house.

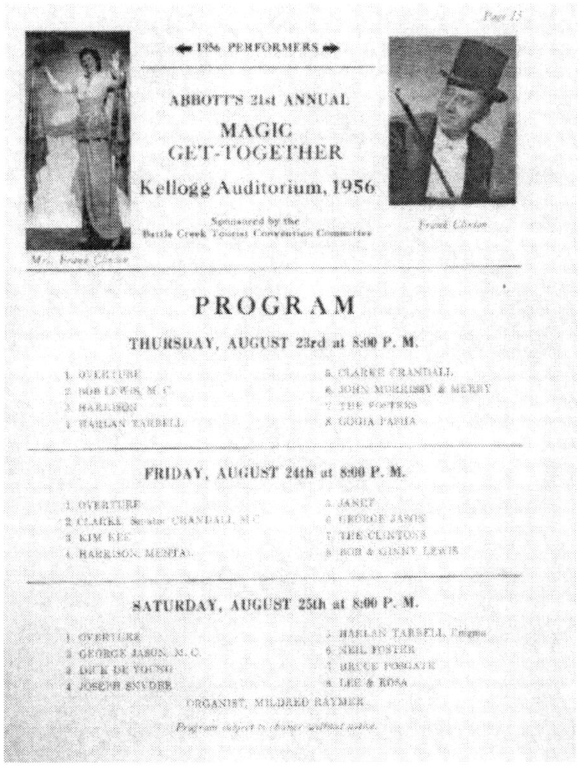

Page 13

1956 PERFORMERS

ABBOTT'S 21st ANNUAL

MAGIC GET-TOGETHER

Kellogg Auditorium, 1956

Sponsored by the Battle Creek Tourist Convention Committee

Mrs. Frank Clinton

Frank Clinton

PROGRAM

THURSDAY, AUGUST 23rd at 8:00 P. M.

1. OVERTURE
2. BOB LEWIS, M.C.
3. HARRISON
4. HARLAN TARBELL
5. CLARKE CRANDALL
6. JOHN MORRISSY & MERRY
7. THE FOSTERS
8. GOGIA PASHA

FRIDAY, AUGUST 24th at 8:00 P. M.

1. OVERTURE
2. CLARKE Senator CRANDALL, M.C.
3. KIM KEE
4. HARRISON, MENTAL
5. JANET
6. GEORGE JASON
7. THE CLINTONS
8. BOB & GINNY LEWIS

SATURDAY, AUGUST 25th at 8:00 P. M.

1. OVERTURE
2. GEORGE JASON, M.C.
3. DICK DE YOUNG
4. JOSEPH SNYDER
5. HARLAN TARBELL, Enigma
6. NEIL FOSTER
7. BRUCE POSGATE
8. LEE & ROSA

ORGANIST, MILDRED RAYMER

Program subject to change without notice.

Program showing Janet and The Clintons as two separate acts

3: Tale of the Goldbach Boat House

"Vice Adm. (Ret.) B.L. Stabile
President - Webb Institute of Naval Architecture Aug 28, 1989

Dear Ben:

Thank you for your letter of August 16. The name on the boat house should be "The Goldbach Boat House".

Regards, Richard A. Goldbach

I always considered the "Webb Boat House" on Long Island Sound to be my "Normandy Invasion" site for courting Janet. Rob, in his role as Webb Trustee, exploited the vulnerability of his twin's possessiveness of the Boat House by establishing an extravagant contribution amount for the right to name it. The contribution Rob demanded was large enough to reconstruct the Webb Boat House more than five times over.

Then, Rob came back for even more money for new boats.

4: Tale of Janet Naming Speede Drydock in Romania

When the time for christening Speede Drydock came, I was approached by the President of Daewoo Mangalia Shipyard, who said, "You're not thinking about anyone except Mrs. Goldbach, are you? The word is out on her in Romania and my workers want to meet her."

So, Janet was unanimously selected as Godmother for the Naming Ceremony of Speede Drydock in Mangalia, Romania on May 10, 2002. As Godmother, Janet wielded the ax that cut the rope that smashed the traditional christening bottle of champagne against the hull of Speede.

When the 850 foot long Speede Drydock was transported to Norfolk, aboard MV Blue Marlin, it was the largest single piece of cargo that had ever been transported by ship in the history of the world.

"I am grateful to represent the many highly skilled individuals from three continents and three proud cultures who have joined together to create this vessel which I am honored to name. This vessel has very unique status as the very first ship drydocking facility in the entire world to be designed and constructed in the twenty first century.

It is also the only such facility that meets the extraordinary environmental and competitive demands of the twenty first century. It is the world's first facility to be classified a ship painting environmentally encapsulated depot.

This unique classification, as abbreviated, provides the name this magnificent vessel will carry as it brings credit to its creators and honor and good fortune to its owners throughout the century ahead.

I name this vessel Speede"

Anul V • Nr 96 • 17 mai 2002 5000 lei

Mangalia

Bilunar de opinie și informație

Șantierul DAEWOO:

pag. 16

SPEEDE - primul doc ecologic din lume lansat la apa

Mangalia news coverage of naming ceremony by Janet

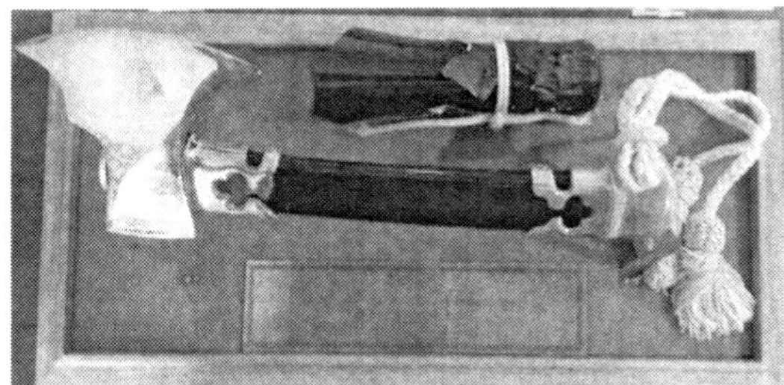

Janet's Speede Christening Axe

5: Tales of Janet at Packer Collegiate Institute

From Rich to the Richmond Theater: Attention Ms. Karin Gartzke, Chief Executive, February 13, 2003

"Dear Ms. Gartzke:

My wife Janet and I recently attended Richmond for the first time. In addition to being most impressed by the performance of "Blue Room" and magnificence of the facility we were drawn, as I'm sure many others are, to the thoughtful and inspiring words on the keystone over the stage i.e. "to wake the soul by tender strokes of art".

It happens that Janet and I are sponsoring the new Janet Clinton Performing Arts Center at Packer Collegiate Institute in New York City. Packer is one of the most if not the most prestigious private schools in the city. My wife attended Packer for thirteen years. She and I credit those years for much of the good that has come into our lives. Because of that and Janet's long and successful career as a professional performer, we are excited to be a part of Packer's development of its significantly expanded performing arts facilities and program.

Janet and I both believe that the words over your stage can inspire the youth of Packer. We therefore request your organization consider giving Packer permission to use them and/or endorsing that use properly attributed to the historic Richmond Theater and their originator, who Maggie Webster advised was Alexander Pope of nearby Twickenham.

Thank you for considering this request.

Best regards,
Richard Goldbach
16 Hale House, 34 DeVere Gardens, London, W85AQ

From Richmond Theatre/Kate Jarvis to Rich, February 19, 2003

Dear Mr. Goldbach,

We would be delighted to give permission for you to use the saying provided it is properly accredited to Richmond Theatre and Alexander Pope. I am not sure how you would go about getting permission on behalf of Mr. Pope as, obviously, he died in 1744. This may be something you need to look into.

We would be interested to hear any progress.

Kind regards,

Kate
Kate Jarvis,
Administrator, Richmond Theatre, The Green, Richmond, Surrey TW9 1QJ

Richard Goldbach Talk at Packer Collegiate Institute on May 3, 2003

"I'm here because my beautiful wife Janet spent her thirteen most formative years here half a century ago. I feel as out of place here since I am expected to say something worthy of your time, as I did on my first visit in May 1956.

I hoped then as I hope now that I could get through the occasion without embarrassing myself. All I can remember from that original visit is a blur of sophisticated teenage girls with bloodshot eyes they blamed on homework dancing around a Maypole and twirling in white crinoline dresses - like in my Child's Book of Nursery Rhymes.

Not a very good insight into an institution which was to ultimately have such a profound impact on my life. Let's hope I do better now than I did then since a bunch of those same sophisticated girls – no longer teenagers – are here watching me and hoping I get it right this time.

Whatever relationship each of us has with Packer, I believe there are four premises we can agree on:

First, the future of this planet hangs in a fragile balance.

Second, this future will be determined by how well the youth nurtured in this century understand and implement the lessons of the last four thousand years.

Third, the youth who reside in this great nation will have the best opportunity to make an enduring difference in this future.

Finally, in order to make a difference, they will need leadership with extraordinary traits of character.

My observations of Janet over the past forty-eight years convince me that Packer is up to the awesome task of producing an important share of that leadership.

My life, measured by any standard, has been extraordinarily fulfilling. Most of that life, I've taken success for granted. But some years ago, I began to wonder about it.

I was surprised to discover that each experience that ultimately led to fulfillment had been preceded by a life crisis that had threatened permanent setback.

I was also surprised to find that the character traits that I relied on to find my way through each of the crises had not been in my bag of tricks before I encountered Janet. Each had been absorbed from her presence in my life without me being aware of it or giving her any credit for it.

I am now absolutely convinced that Janet's character traits which enabled me to steer through my life came complete with the package I met in 1955 and married in 1960. I am also certain that they are a result of nurturing by her parents and thirteen years at Packer in a way that I cannot discern where Packer leaves off and Janet begins.

While few can measure up to Janet in execution, her character traits have been subtly but firmly reinvested in everyone whose life she has touched and especially her family, her thousands of audiences, the first graders she taught and the artists she paints with.

Those traits include compassion for the feelings of others, respect for different opinions of others, respect for different capabilities of others, civility, humility, persistence, hard work, compulsion to always do her best, reverence for the truth and a truly incredible sense of humor that can lift a room.

Because I concluded that Janet's character is the foundation that my life was built upon and that what Janet stands for is indistinguishable from what Packer stands for, I also had to conclude that Packer was an essential part of my own success.

So here I am to share that conclusion with you.

The fundamental Packer values established by the founding parents of Packer, continued by Dr. Paul Schaeffer and the faculty during Janet's childhood, and carried on by Geoff Pearson and his staff, will continue through the chain of lives touched by Packer for as long as those values attract support.

As they do, they will compete with barbaric forces that challenge advanced civilization.

My father was born in New York City in 1907 even though his par-

ents lived on a farm in Poughkeepsie where my grandfather worked as a farmhand and my grandmother worked as a domestic. So were his three siblings in the following five years.

Several years ago, I asked my Aunt Ruth about the disparity assuming it had something to do with medical care. I will always remember her reply.

"Your grandmother was convinced that New York City was the greatest city in the world in the greatest nation in the world. Being born there was the one gift she was determined to give each of her children."

Ninety-six years later, I'm sure few here would disagree with my grandmother. Certainly, those who seek to acquire power by destroying the power of civilization don't. Why else would they target New York City for the sneak attack which took momentary advantage of Civilization's trust in and dependence on the inherent goodness of mankind?

The purpose of the Packer construction around us is to create the finest urban campus in New York City.

Like you, I do not know where the ideas and ideals will come from in the contest to be waged between the forces defending Civilization and the forces seeking to empower themselves by destroying Civilization.

I am convinced that these ideas and ideals are what Packer provides in its graduation package. Given that, I like the chances of one or more of the youth attracted to and nurtured within this finest urban campus in this greatest city in the world in this greatest nation in the world playing a decisive role in the conflict.

That's something that Janet and I find to be very exciting and something we want to be a part of.

We are especially honored for Janet to be associated with Packer's Performing Arts program since the performing arts, which are the most ancient and universal means of reinvesting the lessons of humanity, have dominated Janet's successes and our life together.

I am also extremely grateful for this opportunity to convey to Janet, the awe I feel for her accomplishments as a performer and extraordinary human being and further to place her incredible lifetime accomplishments before her fellow travelers at Packer.

Thank you for bearing witness to the occasion in this beautiful chapel which, since the first day she entered Packer, has been one of Janet's most special places on Earth.

6: Tale of Madame Helene Champrigand

Janet loves the nation and language of France. During our numerous visits there, because of her fluency in French, she is frequently mistaken for a Parisienne. This brings her much joy and satisfaction. She credits Madam Helene Champrigand, a direct descendant of Voltaire, with this special dimension of her life. Janet learned French from "Champi" during each of her last six years at Packer. In 1958, Janet traveled to France for twelve weeks with Champi, rarely speaking anything but French.

The Packer Magazine – Summer 2008

Goldbach/Chambrigand Scholarship Established

Janet Clinton Goldbach '58 and her husband, Richard Goldbach, have established The Janet Clinton Goldbach '58 Scholarship in Memory of Madame Helene Champrigand.

The Goldbach/Champrigand Scholarship will be awarded to the student completing the junior year at Packer who has the highest grade- point average in French. The student must be completing his or her third year of French study in Packer's Upper School. The award will be made in the form of tuition reduction in the senior year. Annabelle Baylin '09 received the inaugural award in May 2008.

"Champi," a beloved member of the Packer faculty, taught here for the last 17 of her 39 years in the classroom and retired in 1968. She was Mrs. Goldbach's French teacher in high school. Madame Champrigand chaperoned many Packer students on summer trips to France. Before coming to Packer, Madame Champrigand taught at the Shipley School and the Brierley School.

Head of School Dr. Bruce Denis said, "This generous gift will memorialize Madame Champrigand, boost the school's endowment, and provide motivation to our French scholars. Once again, we are most grateful to Janet and Rich Goldbach."

The perpetual scholarship is being established with gifts totaling $135,000 over a seven-year period. Mrs. Goldbach is pleased that this scholarship will continue to be awarded annually, "thus continuing Cham-

pi's presence at Packer."

The Goldbachs have been loyal and generous supporters of Mrs. Goldbach's alma mater. They are also members of the Pelican Society, and they made a major gift to Packer's Building on Success capital campaign. The Janet Clinton Performing Arts Center at Packer is named in honor of Mrs. Goldbach, who had a decades-long career as a professional magician, which began when she was a student at Packer.

....

Dear Mr. and Mrs. Goldbach,

My name is Kristin Howell and I am this year's recipient of the Janet Clinton Goldbach '58 Scholarship. Thank you for funding this scholarship to support the students who love the French language at Packer.

I have been taking French since I was in third grade and have had the privilege to travel to Paris with a few of my peers. I have developed a great respect for the language and the culture that it is deeply rooted in.

Words cannot express my gratitude for your generous donation. I hope to graduate Packer and use my passion for language and literature to create a career for myself.

With gratitude, Kristin

....

Mrs. Janet C. Goldbach '58

Dear Janet and Rich

It is my pleasure to inform you that Wing Moulton '18 has been chosen as this year's recipient of The Janet Clinton Goldbach '58 Scholarship in Memory of Madame Helene Champrigand.

Wing reads at an advanced level and is adept at retaining details, identifying complex ideas, and making connections between texts. Both his careful commentary during discussions and the fluidity of his written work demonstrate the deep critical thinking of a young intellect.

We are very proud of Wing and I hope you find him an appropriate recipient of this very generous scholarship.

Sincerely, Bruce L. Dennis, Head of School

7: Tales of Miracles with Janet

"Dear Janet

Miracles

As I sit in my favorite seat on my favorite couch in my favorite room gazing at my favorite painting of my favorite fellow creature, I marvel at the trillions of things that had to occur in specific sequence in order for me to encounter you, then convince you to agree to join forces with me. Who, in their wildest imagination, could have imagined the lifetime of experiences that would result from that teaming.

Children-Magic Performances-Fulfilling Job Assignments-Jointly Overcoming Adversity-Artistic Endeavors-Public Service-Recognition-Honors-Inventions-World Travel-Grandchildren-Beautiful Homes-Beautiful Works of Art-Prolonged Health (knock on wood)-London Life-Performing Arts-Help for Needy Others, all the direct result of our agreement to pursue life as a couple.

Our agreement to wed turned out to be the foundation of everything good that has happened to me since. Yet, if my Dad hadn't gone to work for General Precision for three short years following the war, he wouldn't have met the bright young man that told him about Webb.- If I hadn't had a smart twin, I wouldn't have been accepted - If the faculty had flunked me first term Freshman year (as they easily could have), I wouldn't have been at Webb in April 1955 - If our 1941 Ford had been working that weekend, I wouldn't have hitched a ride with Reub -If I hadn't hitched a ride with Reub, I wouldn't have met Barbie - If Barbie hadn't been such a busybody, she wouldn't have found I was looking for dates in the city - If you had gone on your Folk's magic show that night, I wouldn't have ever met you - If you hadn't invited us in for coffee, I wouldn't have met your Father - If I hadn't met your father, I wouldn't have had the color wheel with your telephone number - If you had spelled naval with an a instead of an e, I wouldn't have had the opportunity to write a letter to tease you -If - If - If -If - If -If - If - Where might it had ended with a single piece of the puzzle in another place?

The fact that it didn't certainly qualifies as a miracle."

I absolutely knew, when I married you, that the sublime powerful attraction towards you I felt , was a love that would last a lifetime. How wrong I was! The love that will last a lifetime hadn't begun to make itself known. The incredibly strong attraction that I was feeling, was merely intense admiration and respect, made more urgent by sexual attraction.

Seven is the luckiest number. Seven squared = 49, the super luckiest number of all. I am indeed the luckiest creature on Earth for having you as a life partner for those same years. Seven times seven begins to describe the way my love for you has grown.

Still feelings intensely felt,

Rich

8: Tales at Christmas of Life with Janet

Compassionate listener; sage advisor; head-turning beauty; charm of the universe: intellectual champion; persistent doer-of-everything to perfection; magical pied piper extraordinaire; astonishing painter of everything using every style, medium and material; expert wardrobe selector and conserver, gold medal winner for dining room knife/fork manipulation; the single person everyone absolutely knows is their best friend; world's foremost expert in taxi-driving French; most beloved and respected daughter, wife, mom and grandma; all-in-all a pretty good gal.

1939 Enters world with much to make up for after causing maximum discomfort during pregnancy. Becomes first human to have perfect recall of departing the womb.

1940 Becomes youngest child to ride a pony and remember every moment of it.

1947 Becomes youngest child to perform on TV while humiliating other talent contest competitors. Has photo posted in Broadway window for 40 years.

1948 Publicized in Weekly Reader and American Girl periodicals.

1948 to 1956: Assumes persona of "Sweetheart" at all magic conventions.

1955: Performs first platonic experiment on human male subject at Webb Boat House, takes comprehensive notes, abandons experiment for two years; Originates first thank-you note ever received at Webb Institute of Naval Architecture – advises that Webb has been spelling Navel incorrectly for 100 years. Rich considers it a curiosity; Observes first fistfight at a Coney Island bar; learns not to wear wool dresses to square dances.

1956: Neck grows three inches in 12 months.

1957: Makes first appearance as a beautiful swan at Yuletide Ball.

Spectators gasp; Makes first appearance as a beautiful swan in red dress; Rich melts; Decorates first nudist Christmas tree; Issues first of many turn-downs.

1958 Departs for France on the Il de France; Has picture taken on sled, Picture still being used to lure tourists for forty years, Returns to U.S. after 12 weeks. Celebrates with first jelly glass of champagne R starts New London to Tufts weekly commutes,

1959: J issues first of many maybe-maybe nots at Saranac; R meets Roquie, J sees shooting star at Minnewaska, issues then retracts first "yes"; Looks great in Impala Bat mobile; R keeps commuting, J falls for "last straw" tunnel fantasy, finalizes yes; Injures Cape Cod geezer with lobster shell in the process of getting bolder; Gets two turkeys for Thanksgiving plus a Gimbals' setting for a Clinton gem. Wears ring-out-for-repair sign when Clinton gem falls out of cheap Gimbals" prongs, Rodgers Lake dip.

R's Marriage Memories 1960 to 1977: Married by Chance, a minister with a sex-education fetish, Tommy Dillon sings, R and J make loud vows; J's beauty brings tears to eyes of mystery derelict that sends bowl of flowers. Scores perfect 10 in "Hitting-bride-on-Head-with-Bouquet"; Hides garter where no one will find it; Waldorf Room 2323 placed permanently out-of–service; Happy couple stays at Mountain Lake Hotel but spends honeymoon at Homestead, Tennis match becomes comedy act of the season, Bingo cards bring new Christmas card friends from Kentucky that need orthodontist assistance, Let the Dirty Dancing begin. A foreboding future looms when R doesn't stop for dozen-dozen buttons and smelling flowers, Tears turn the tide.

1960 Noank: Aunt Marian, Uncle Muriel. Gretel, Hansel, Pete (what R ya doin?), delectable parakeets, dog poop, hair balls (something's done something), de-fleaing Hansel, de-mangeing Gretel, Heidi jumps on R's head, finds home, Black spots turn out to move, Long flea baths ahead, R's pumpkin spill, Hansel takes a filthy swim, Edible electrical pencil sharpeners, how do you spell Pequannock Bridge, Mimeographs, Purple fingers, Tears, New vocabulary, Show and tell surprises, First grade sex education, Snow man with two smiling fac-

es, Pumpkins galore from Ron's garden, Orange potato salad, Butter on everything, Lobsters from Abbott's, 35 cents a pound, Main line train whistles, Sterling arrives for Christmas.

1961 Noank: Contract bridge, Manhattans, Beckett Hill, Hula hoop, 1812 Symphony, Jazz, Big Beat on the Organ, Mystic fire, Shrimp jambalaya by the pail, Beef stroganoff by the pail, butter on nothing, Egg diet, Flu fun, Welcome home daddy, Morning sickness, Second-hand maternity clothes, Outee, Breathing exercises, Underutilized shower, Gretel leaps into snow drift, Hansel falls out of window, R installs world's longest second-story pulley clothes line, Kristen arrives, Dr. Verie excels, Cleft lip, Syringes, Diaper, Gretel in heat, Neighborhood dogs help us move.

1961 Gales Ferry: George Foote, Ken McBride (dress it up) Dead Man's Curve, Diaper service, Clothes drier, Grass growing in basement thanks to Gretel, Portulacca, Milk-man negotiation, Fireplace fires, Hansel dive-bombs rare orange Chinese bowl, Christmas in MD with Sterling, Doug excels with top, Uncle Franklin rats on him.

1962 to 1965 Gales Ferry: Dr McCullough, Boston Children's, Cleft palette found, trip home, R sick, Heavy snow, J lost No money, No windshield wiper, Helpful strangers, K blowing, K Baptism in Brooklyn, Christmas at 290, Grampy performs hank to cane, Doug tries too (it's getting harder), Grampy premiers as Santa, Diaper service, Clothes drier, Picture window, Ice skating, Push Kristen in sleigh, Gretel chases old ladies' dogs, Donald and Daphne, Rats love corn, Gretel runs from horse, Ann Vance, Eileen, Contract bridge with Coopers, Family choo-choo with Kristen, Swing-o matic, Opal, Cleft palette time, Kristen left all alone, Bear (Mur), Swing on carport, Gretel runs after squirrels but passes them all, May, Claire, Walt, Ocean View Park, Assistant Shipwright Superintendent, Hillman, swimming hole, Vality, Methodist church, Christmas candlelight service, K Christmas cards, Weekends at 290, Devils Hop yard, Pete catches cold, Mustang arrives.

1965-1967 Cohasset: Motel, Digging clams, Nantasket, Pizza, House-on-hill, Tufts reunion, Stan and Ellie, Rustic Drive, Ledge,

Black Rock House, Fishing, Soft shell clam digging, Friends for Kristen, Unitarian Church, Janet's candle Christmas, Space trolley, Miscarriage, Ice show, Top hat and tails, Pixie costumes, Legonis, Theatrical photographs, Brochures, Blizzard, Janet's IBM debut, Rich too, You do as I do, Vista Cruiser, Hancock Hall, K's foot wave, Cathedral in the Pines, Janet's Thermometer, Bingo, If those kids only knew what is behind those Pixie points, Pixie clap, EXPO 66, Sterling's missing leg, To the head of the line with wheelchair, Rabbit Hill, Morning sickness, April 18, Breast feeding, Ricky bites, J pulls it back, Ricky learns lesson, Ducker's rocking chair, How do you spell Pascagoula?, J does SAM Convention show.

1967 Dauphine Island: Rich comes back late, Mosquitoes, mosquitoes, mosquitoes, Kristen discovers how to make Ricky happy, Country club pool.

1967 to 1971 Suzanne Circle: Country Club Estates, George Wallace Fund Raiser, Rot School, uniforms, Carpooling, Pat Bloom, Irving, Grace Lutheran Church, Ricky Baptism, Space Trolley II, Mardis Gras, MOT, Fort Morgan picnic, Oceanfront lots for sale, Haddow and Sims, Clyde Ewing, Fettermans, Mobile Symphony, R stands for "Dixie", J sits, Grandma/Grampy arrive, Grandma puffs on K's flower, Warm Gulf water, Ralph-Diane, Herring original, House and lot hunting.

1971 to 1977 Bit & Spur Road: Heidi, Mother Cat, Tiger, Puffka, Puffka's baby dogs, Puffka's baby kittens, Grampy as Santa. Grampy becomes Doctor of philosophy and ordained minister of Church of Holy Light, Grampy invests in bells, Grampy loves carrying Mother Cat in wheelbarrow, Grampy and Twinkle toes, Pixie's black magic, Pixie's Christmas marathons in churches, Coast Guard helicopter hanger, Schools, Homes, Migraine headaches, J leaps interstate highway fence in top hat, tails and opera hose, J meets Mayor, National Magic Week sign, Pixie becomes household name, Dauphin way Methodist church, K's bell choir, R/J weekends in New Orleans, Oyster bars, Dress shopping, Nap, La Ruth's, Your Fathers' Mustache, beer, peanuts, Al Hurt, Pete Fountain, Fats Domino, Bourbon Street,

Breakfast at Brennen's, Milk punches, feeling numb, back to reality with Pizza, St. Louis and Kansas City, SAM magic contests, K cooking, K schmoozing Duke Stern, Ricky breaks up Atlanta comedy show, Ricky sells balloon animals at art fair, Ricky calms Santa during helicopter arrival, New Orleans magic convention, Duke Stern and Jay Marshall and Karroll Foxx poke fun at J, Isn't Magic Dauphin Way Methodist church K's bell choir, swimming at the Y, family weekends at Gulf Shores, Ricky trailing five girls, Ricky ducking Blue Angels, Crab catching, J's shark heroes run for it, Wild Turkey, Whiskey sours and milk punches, Where do the weekends go?, Square dancing, Fontana Dam, Horse-back riding, Grand Juries, Bingo Stant, Henry Swanner, R's high blood pressure, R is fired, J saves R, Pugh Roberts, Ken Cooper,

With extraordinary joy, admiration, gratitude, attraction and, above all love,

Rich

9: Tale of a 50 – Year Anniversary Celebration

Janet on July 22, 2010 at 50th Anniversary Reception

July 23, 2010

To Our Beloved Friends and Family Members,

Fifty years is the recognized milestone for fulfilling the all-important pledges the two of us made to each other on July 23, 1960, when we commenced our married life together. Thank you for enriching our celebration of that milestone by joining us this weekend.

In our innocence, when we made our pledges, we thought only of the life adventure ahead. We had no concept of the obstacles to surviving intact that we would ultimately encounter.

In our innocence, we were convinced the support that we would get from each other, would be all we would need to confront any challenges. We gave no thought to what else would ultimately have to come from the presence of others in our lives.

We rejoice this milestone weekend knowing we often made it by the skin of our teeth only because of some kind of timely boost that came from others. You, who have honored us by joining us this weekend, are among those who provided those necessary and welcome boosts.

For that and for your continuing friendship, we give you the love that comes from knowing each of you is an integral part of the couple that the outside world knows as Janet and Rich Goldbach. We hope you derive joy and satisfaction from that knowledge just as we do.

Gratefully and lovingly, Janet & Rich

Rich and Janet on July 23, 2010 at 50th Anniversary Banquet

10: Ken's Tale of 50 Years Celebration

Dear Janet and Rich,

You were perfect hosts for everyone at your celebration, but you really made the two of us feel most special throughout the weekend. We left with so many good memories....

...serendipitously meeting you and Janet and Lura at the Inn Friday...learning Lura & Vita are 'cousins'...the lovely suite at the Inn...the corsages...the notes tied in bows...the valet parking and motor car swooshing us around...the picnic, Clyde S. Dale, the boat ride (with Liz & Tommy & Lydia—Lydia patted the seat beside her & said to Ken, "you can sit here"...Janet, your guided tour of your exquisite home and beautiful paintings – particularly the Lady of Shallot (which is also special to us – see the enclosed Tennyson poem to which Ken added verses for us)...Vita's photo tour with Barbie and the statues (some photos here for you, too)...and Rich, I can't remember a happier sweeter time than the hours we spent with you at the dining table Saturday.

What a joy for us to meet so many new friends – all of them in your honor, and we are honored to be among them. As we said when departing, you gave us wonderful life memories from the whole weekend!

Our most sincere thanks and love, Ken & Vita

Rich and Ken day of July 23, 2010

Part IV –Tales of Others

Who Influenced Me

Rich, Franklin and Rob

1: Tale of Rob

Rob is my identical twin. He is the dominant twin. I heard once that twin dominance is caused by the twin nearest the womb exit before birth annoying the twin hunched up in the back of the womb by stretching out and occupying more than his/her fair share of space. According to that theory, womb comfort leads the outer twin to a life of being laid back while womb discomfort leads the inner twin to a life of ambition. Whether the theory is valid or not, it sure fits my view of Rob and me.

I do not know when I started remembering things. Probably somewhere between the ages of two and four. From the beginning of my thinking, I always knew when Rob was there and when he wasn't. When he wasn't, an integral part of me that I expected to look out for me was missing. We were inseparable during childhood and that's probably why.

Rob was the smartest twin, the most popular twin, the fastest twin, the best baseball hitter, the best football player and the boss twin. I was the twin that took orders, the funniest twin and to some, the cutest twin. Life was good. Life was between Rob and me on one side and everyone else on the other side.

My parents were glad we were always looking out for each other. Our big brother Franklin was frustrated by where this left him in the sibling rivalry competition. He did his best to play Rob and me off each other, but it seldom worked.

Until we were 21, we did the same things, slept in the same bedroom, played with the same friends, had the same teachers, played the same games, pulled the same pranks, played the same sports, went to the same parties, went to the same church services, drove the same car, double-dated, went to the same college and took the same courses. It didn't matter to me that I was in Rob's shadow because that still left me ahead of almost everyone else.

Rob and Rich's first job, paying 75 cents per month (second row 2 & 3)

July 12, 1958, when we both graduated from Webb Institute, changed all of that. We both headed off to different states and different employers. We were soon to be working in completely different lines of work and be living with wives instead of each other. Rob could no longer look out after me. We attended different churches and came to different theological conclusions. Robs conclusions were more traditional than mine, although I rarely discussed mine with others.

Need for such changes eventually takes place in every sibling relationship. But, since Rob's and my relationship was so close from the beginning and lasted 21 years, the adjustment required by us was much more extensive and difficult than it was for many other siblings.

Rob published a book after he retired in which he discussed his theological conclusions. He discussed the book and its conclusions with his classmates by email. This discussion was far more important than any previous discussion among the classmates. Even though I felt it best to avoid discussing my own particular theological conclusions, I wanted to participate in it.

"From: Richard A. Goldbach
Sent: Sunday, April 24, 2011 4:20 PM

To: Robert Goldbach; ; Charles Grover;
Subject: Friends

Thank you, Rob, for stimulating this extraordinary exchange with your thought provoking book.

Thank you, Dan, Charlie, Bud and John, for honoring me by including me as a friend during the exchange.

How I wish I could, armed with your insights and the wisdom I accumulated during the years, go back and earn that honor.

It will have to suffice to tell you that I now understand and fully appreciate that each and every one of our individual unique human characteristics was put there by Creation (Physics) and/or a Creator (Theology) for some essential, often long-forgotten, purpose".

Love, Rich

Apparently, my email caused some confusion and concern and became a topic of discussion between some of our classmates and Rob. Presumably, Rob sent this email to our Webb Classmates on April 25, 2011 in an effort to clarify my intentions.

"Rich and I don't see much of each other and haven't for a number of years. I would probably broad brush the reasons by saying we just don't have in common what we once did including all of our family, now gone. When I received my copy of his message below to many of you I tried with my special "twin" skills to get "behind" what he was trying to communicate.

Clearly, he sees and appreciates what many of us are recognizing at this point in our lives and after all these years, namely the experience that we shared fifty years ago was extraordinary and lasting. Just as clearly, he sees that despite the great stress that impacted our individual relationships at the time, the trust, respect and affection between us has stood the test of time and distance.

What you may not appreciate, and what I think Rich is trying to say is that he is especially moved by the thought of these shared experiences and relationships, and they mean as much or more to him than whatever more traditional rewards have come his way.

You may be aware that Rich has achieved significant business and financial success. He would never tell you but I think you should know that his hand has been largely responsible for his success and none of it has come easily.

Early in the 1970s shortly after Rich left Electric Boat to join Litton, Litton became the target of a federal criminal investigation for activities where Rich had no responsibility. Rather than defending the action Litton found it convenient to distort the action to make it appear that Rich was solely culpable and then leave Rich to defend himself. I can scarcely conceive how alone Rich must have felt trying to defend himself against wrongful government charges without any assistance from his employer.

Long story short Rich nonetheless prevailed and moved on to be President of Metro Machine Corp., a small and very ordinary Norfolk ship repairer when he joined them. Virtually on his own and without any fear of being a "bull in a china shop" he instituted business, technical and bidding procedures that turned Metro into a very highly regarded contractor and earned it the honor of "Small Business Company of the Year" which he accepted in a Rose Garden ceremony. It's not easy to achieve financial success dealing with the Navy and the US Government but Rich accomplished it in spades. Unfortunately for him he appears to be irreplaceable so he will probably die with his boots on.

Rich has been extremely generous with his wealth but you wouldn't know it because he chooses anonymity. He has been particularly generous when people of talent need a hand up and he has made a huge difference in many lives. I haven't exactly been a slouch when it comes to making money but I'm sure Rich has given away more than I have earned in my lifetime.

I just thought you should know.

Rob

Comment:

My email message was written at the time Janet and I first knew with certainty that, after 25 years, we were finally out from under our personal guarantees of the significant bank financing necessary to operate Metro Machine as a 100% employee-owned company. After 24 years, we finally knew that there was no chance a company financial failure would inevitably lead to a Goldbach family financial failure. I had finally achieved my life's ambition of arranging a sale of the stock of the Metro Machine ESOP at a price that greatly benefited the workers who, however reluctantly, had placed their trust in me.

I was euphoric and I think it showed in my email. My high-risk fulfilling and exciting ordeal was finally behind me and I had met all the obligations I had incurred in the process. I had played the extraordinary hand I had been dealt and, amazingly, I had won!

I did not need or want to try to convince anyone, except myself, about the reasons for my theological conclusions. But, I did very much want to participate in the extraordinary discussion that was taking place, because it was such an important classmate occasion and because Rob's book had triggered it.

Realizing how blessed I now knew I was in my work and assuming some of our classmates also realized it, I joined the discussion by making several observations I considered important. These statements conveyed my high regard for my classmates and my gratitude for the extraordinary gifts I now knew I had received from life.

I can now see how some came to think my comments came from "out of the blue", but they really did come after a lot of thought.

Six months later, the news of my sale of Metro Machine to General Dynamics became public knowledge for the first time.

From Rich to his Webb Classmates – November 2011

Dear All,

Big news for me is the fact that, on October 31, 2011, I sold the stock owned by Metro's Employee Stock Ownership Plan (ESOP) to General Dynamics for $165 million after paying all transactional expenses. I implemented this ESOP for the purpose of borrowing $17 million to purchase the Metro Machine stock then owned by my partner.

Between 1987 and now, the Metro ESOP had already paid out $52 million in retirement and death benefits. In addition to paying off the original $17 million loan, the ESOP will be returning $217 million to Metro's 500 employees and retirees. It is the satisfaction of a lifetime to witness the pride and excitement Metro employees are deriving from this accomplishment.

Meanwhile, it pleases me greatly that Electric Boat, where you (Pete

Hall – Class Rep), Ron, Ed and I began our life after Webb, thinks enough of my life at Metro to add Metro to its prior acquisitions of Bath and NASSCO. I will be retiring from shipbuilding on October 31, excepting duties to be performed under a three-year consulting agreement with GD, and other duties performed as Trustee for the ESOP.

That means I will be leaving to younger others the important work of carrying on the extraordinary life of William Webb. However, I am putting the finishing touches on a complete restoration and modernization of the original 1841 farmhouse and barn that are located on the 138 acre Suffolk, Virginia farm where Janet's and my own residence is located. These 1841 buildings and the 138 acres will comprise more than half of the original Cherry Grove Plantation with British occupation dating back to the late 1600s and Nansemond Indian Tribe Ancestral Hunting Grounds dating back to the time of Christ.

With the spirits of those past occupiers, an abundance of deer, other wildlife and birds of innumerable species; I have a lot of company, even when I'm the only living human on the premises.

Janet, who continues to enjoy her avocation of painting, sends her best. We have two children and eight grandchildren, all living locally, that we see as often as they want to see us.

From Rob to Rich June, 22, 2014

Rich

We had to hit the road for what turned to be a seven-hour drive (into the setting sun no less). On top of our two from NJ to Webb.......haven't done that for a while.

No one who heard your speech had any doubt that you deserved your doctorate. It had a great message spoken well and from the heart. I was very proud of you.

We are already in the sing at Chautauqua......Imagine attending worship every day in a 2000 seat usually full open air amphitheater.

I'll try to call after my knee surgery July 1

Rich and Rob, Rob's last moments as an unmarried twin September 1958

2: Tales of Franklin

From Frank to Rob and Rich February 2, 2003

Dear Rob and Rich,

In the past several months, I have been made aware of how important my family is to me. I've been honored all my life to have the greatest brothers a man could have. I know that in the past I haven't shown this. You have both made my life extremely comfortable.

Now with Karen in my life, taking care of me, my life is just about full.

I want to thank you and your great wives for all the kind things you have done and continue to do. I hope there is enough time left that we may enjoy being close together as brothers.

Thank you again for all you have done for me.

Frank

In my mind, I sometimes see a confused picture of a party taking place on the small front lawn of our house in Scotch Plains, NJ, with people all around me. I don't believe my brief visions could be what they seem to be, because the event envisioned took place when Rob and I were only two, an age my memory doesn't go back to.

There are family pictures and stories about that day that describe it as an accidental party because my parents knew nothing about it until everyone in the neighborhood showed up. Franklin, knowing it was the twins' birthday, had traveled the neighborhood far and wide, inviting everybody to the party he knew should be happening.

Franklin knew my Mom obviously must know because Rob and I were her twins and everyone knows a birthday means party. But, the depression was not yet over so my Mom probably figured, why waste ice cream and cake on two kids who probably aren't quite there yet?

For everyone else, the twins of Park View Drive first birthday party was a pretty big deal, kind of like a solar eclipse, how often can it happen? So, attendance was good, there were plenty of presents, but ice cream and cake were somewhat in short supply.

Franklin was looking after his brothers here before we even knew it. This was something we frequently didn't come to inspire by our two versus one tactics. Even though Franklin could easily outpunch the two of us combined, he was no match for our combined vocal chords. Rob and I screaming in unison, "Mom, he's hitting us," would inevitably bring her over to our side. And when she did, she had the authority to throw him out of the house, providing a victory for the twins.

When that happened, Franklin would use the pity he convinced us to feel for him to win us away from Mom to his side. Sometimes, that resulted in her punishing all three of us just to settle things down. Mom often told about a coat she watched sail past her window on a bitter cold night after she had thrown Franklin out based on our pleadings. The twins were saving Franklin after having him thrown out of the house.

Dad was always working late because of the war effort, so he missed all the four-way fun. Even though some nights took longer, Mom would always prevail eventually. Clearly, the fact that she had many more siblings to practice on than we did gave her an advantage.

I remember the gratitude I felt towards Franklin when he coped, almost alone, with all of the difficulties of the Cancer that brought Dad's life to an end. I was little help. It seems I must have had more time to help than I gave. I tried to make it up to Franklin during his own difficult days but some things are not made to be fixed. The love Franklin and Dad shared was quietly intense but probably never stated.

Franklin was, by a mile, the charmer of the Goldbach brothers and the entire Goldbach clan for that matter. While I envied him that, he seemed to get more long-term grief from that quality than pleasure. He once said, "if I ever mention the word marriage again, please get a gun and shoot me."

Fortunately, he tried marriage one more time with Karen, a four-time loser herself, and hit gold. She was to lovingly nurse him through the travesty of diabetes that ended his life. He was finally able to love someone back. Ironically, diabetes gave him an important gift of life that had otherwise eluded him.

Maybe Franklin had some flaws. Don't we all? But the Franklin that loved Karen had no flaws. And the Franklin that loved his brothers had no flaws.

Franklin had Karen and his brothers and their wives with him the night he died, the last five people in the World he knew loved him without reservation.

There would be no more two on one or one on two tactics. My last words to him the night he died were that I had always been proud to have him as a brother.

Franklin and Rich 1954 in front of the trunk of Frank's Plymouth that Rich ran into a telephone pole and tried to cover up.

3: *Tales of Ruth, Frank and Edgar*

Frank Clinton Oil Painting by Janet Goldbach-Smithfield AC

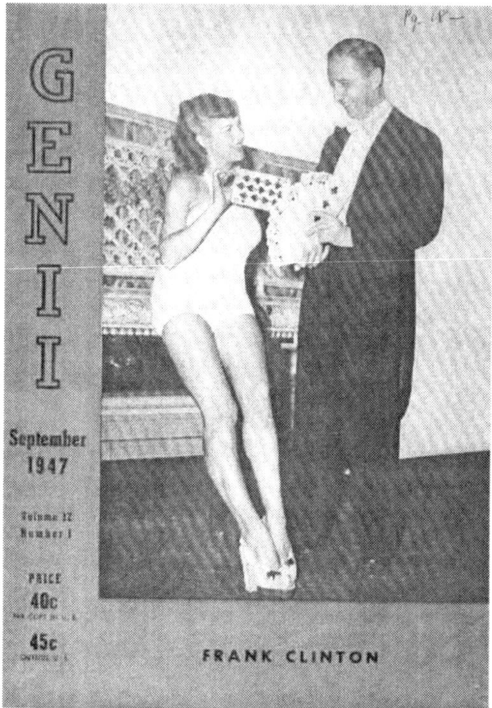

FRANK CLINTON

188 Hicks Street, Brooklyn 2, New York

By JEAN HUGARD

Frank Clinton is another Magician who has achieved Magical heights after his interest was aroused as a small boy when he purchased a ten cent "Ball Vase" in a bicycle shop. From that time on, all his spare dimes and quarters went to buy magic equipment. Later he was taken over to Martinka's by his mother, and today he can describe in detail everything he saw in that small boy's Paradise. He remembers that, being a child, he was not too welcome, and he recalls standing open-mouthed in awe as a large man discussed with the proprietor a floating woman illusion. He finally left with a book—Goldston's Tricks and Illusions, and still has it as a part of his very complete magical library. At the age of ten, he put on his first "formal" show in the conservatory in the rear of a neighbor's home and netted a profit of seven dollars for the neighbor's pet charity. Years later, after a radio appearance, he received a letter from the little girl who was his playmate at the time, and in whose home the show was given, asking if he remembered it.

Frank Clinton today is credited with being one of the busiest of New York's professional performers, being in constant demand for clubs and theatres. He is a fine showman who always gets the greatest entertainment value out of everything he does. He works in a light, friendly style, and is one of the comparatively few magicians who have made a serious study of stagecraft. He is far more interested in knowing how to walk onto a stage, how to leave it, how to acknowledge applause, how to retrieve a fallen object, etc., than in learning a new sleight or pass.

Clinton also has the fortunate and valuable knack of attracting good publicity. For example, on Friday, the 13th of June, he arranged some publicity based on the theme of superstition. In the morning he was on the "Hi-Jinx" program being interviewed by Jinx Falkenburg and Tex McCrary over Station WNBC. A large photo of him (reproduced on the cover) appeared in the afternoon newspaper, and in the evening he was on radio station WNEW. On that day, his publicity reached an estimated audience of over six million people.

Clinton joined the Society of American Magicians in 1927, and has been an active member ever since. He has held numerous offices in the Parent Assembly and was recently elected to its presidency.

He is assisted on the stage by his wife, professionally known as Ruth Andree, and who is secretary of the New York Magigals.

He is planning on breaking his eight-year-old daughter into the act this coming season. She has appeared professionally in television and presented a short magic routine as part of a telecast program. Clinton, himself, has made a number of television appearances and is scheduled for a series of them this fall.

He has done much to advance magic, and is a performer of whom magic may be justly proud.

Frank and Ruth producing Mergie, holding the chosen card he found.

Photos of Ruth's Swedish Mother Kristina and Father Svenning, taken when in their 20s, hang on our living room wall alongside each other in death as they were in life. She is beautiful. He is handsome. She was one of seven siblings who were brought up in a Soldier's cottage not much larger than the size of a tool shed. He was one of eight brothers who lived in a large house with extensive lands presented to the family by a grant from the King.. They met and married in New Britain, CT, something they never could have done in Sweden because of the difference in their classes.

Ruth was Kristina's and Svenning's only child. She taught at Yale University as the Montessori Critic and Demonstration Teacher teaching by the methods she had learned from her professor who had been personally instructed by Madame Montessori. Ricky, Ruth's grandson learned to read "Tip and Mitten" using Madame Montessori's methods.

Frank's Father was also named Frank. He was a successful businessman who owned the New York stores of the Danbury Hat Company. Frank Senior married Etta Olcott, a young lady of leisure living in Brooklyn. The couple gave birth to Frank Junior, Janet's dad, who was born in late 1899 in the family mansion on Park Slope.

When Frank Junior was going through his Father's papers thirty years later, he discovered something he had never known. His father had the same interest in magic that he had. In fact, his father had constructed some magic effects which were his own unique inventions.

So, father and son actually had the common bond of the mysteries of magic, but it was to remain unknown to both of them until one of them died.

Frank's grandmother, Janet Olcott, lived in the mansion with Frank and Etta. Janet Olcott was the given name of the only child of Ruth and Frank.

Frank and Edgar Clinton in 1900

Edgar, Frank's older brother, also lived in the mansion until he was drafted and gassed in the trenches of World War I. Edgar had the makings of an extraordinary portrait artist, like the niece Janet he would never meet. He had art studios on Park Avenue and 5th Avenue in Manhattan. All Edgar's finished portraits have a place on our walls.

Janet and I can see all of Edgar's artwork as we recline in bed. The most important portrays the woman who was the Love of Edgar's Life, sewing. She could well have been sewing when she learned Edgar would not be returning from the trenches. After hearing Edgar was alive when the shooting ended, her momentary plans for having beautiful children with him ended. She had forgotten about the gas!

One day in November 1918, as Frank was stepping off the curb to cross the street in Brooklyn, he had the absolute conviction Edgar had just died. In fact, that was the actual date and time Edgar succumbed to the pneumonia caused by his having been gassed when the shooting was officially over but some fighting continued.

Edgar Clinton's painting of his Love Sewing in Keene Valley, NY

Frank spoke of Edgar frequently and fondly. Edgar's Christening gown hangs right above Frank's in our living room. The gowns are in pristine condition, even though they are now well over 100 years old. Photos of Edgar and Frank wearing the gowns hang nearby.

Edgar has his own pew in Duck Church next to Frank's. It looks out on the Chapel named after his little brother and the woman his little brother married. Edgar's casket flag is on permanent display in our house. Even though Janet and I never knew Edgar, he is an everyday part of our lives. Even though we believe World War I was senseless, we are proud that Edgar served his country when he was called.

When Frank was a teenager, he became fascinated with Vaudeville. He watched the Vaudeville show every Wednesday, always buying a ticket for the same seat for the following Wednesday. Soon after Edgar died, Frank became a banker, later starting his own title abstract company. He originated the concept of title insurance.

Frank traveled to Europe in the 1930s and encountered Ruth, whom he married in 1937. Ruth joined Frank in his magic act, just in time to help Frank provide the USO troop entertainment needed throughout the years of World War II. Since Ruth and Frank were over the age of 40, they were pleased that there was a way for them to serve those who served their country in World War II, as Edgar had in World

War I.

One night, they drove to one of their regular USO locations. They were shuttled off to the back of a waiting vehicle with drawn curtains and driven to a ship that was ready to deploy. The name of the ship was blacked out and, with the drawn curtains, they had no way of knowing where they were.

Their magic apparatus was hoisted aboard with rope hoists and set on the weather deck. It was their turn to come aboard next, so Ruth and Frank, in the formal attire they always wore when performing, climbed up the exterior of the ship on a rope ladder to reach the same weather deck location. Ruth's long gown was hiked up and tied securely by a sailor to avoid its billowing in the brisk breeze that was blowing that night.

The hard work and discipline of the nightly USO shows refined the act of Ruth and Frank Clinton as nothing else could have. Responding to surprises, like they encountered that windy night, prepared Frank to be ready when Janet's big break came along in 1947. Janet was taught to work around any kind of unexpected obstacle whenever she performed for nothing was ever permitted to come in the way of a performance.

After the war, Ruth and Frank continued to be close friends with many of the other star entertainers they had met through the USO, who had also volunteered their services. After one of Frank's shows when the war was over, a sailor from the audience showed Frank a very worn and dog-eared "Big Dollar Bill". He said that Frank had given it to him during a wartime USO show and he had carried it throughout the war, as a good-luck charm to keep him safe.

Frank and Ruth performed thousands of shows. They never missed a show for any reason, because they knew there could always be one person out there who really needed them. "The show must go on" was not just a saying for the Clintons. It was a lifetime commitment that became Janet's, too. And, that commitment applied to every aspect of Janet's life, not just the shows!

The night after Frank's funeral, Stan Romaine, who was sleeping in the bed Frank had used, said that Frank had come to him during the night. Stan wrote down what he heard Frank say and showed it to me at breakfast. The note said, "Please tell them it's going to be OK". It had to be Frank. He would always provide reassurance to anyone who needed it He knew we all needed it that day.

4. Grandchildren

Jared 1995 **Janet 1995**

Sarah 2001 **Katherine 2002**

Amanda 2004

Hunter 2004

Hudson 2009

Trevor 2012

5: Tales of John

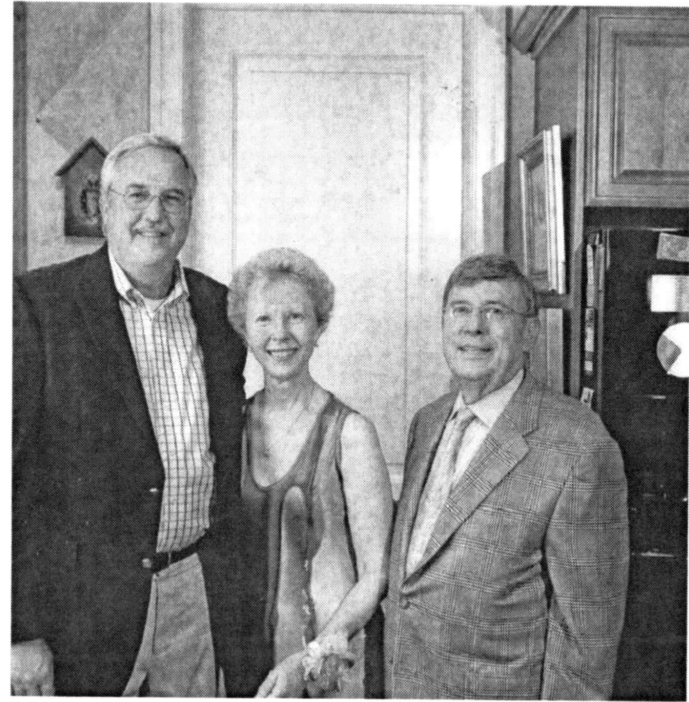

John, Janet and Rich

Metro Machine President John Strem's talk at Rich's retirement dinner:

"Thank you all for coming to this very special retirement dinner honoring Richard. I seldom prepare in writing to speak in front of groups: however, I knew this time it was essential. It was partially driven by the fact that Richard's passion for the industry and his love for Metro left me somewhat unprepared for this event, because I always thought he would be working when it was time for me to retire. Richard's 56 plus years in the industry is both an amazing accomplishment and an incredible contribution. Many people work for decades in an industry and do very well. However, very few people leave an industry that has improved and strengthened based on their contributions the way Richard has, leaving his footprints behind that will always remain.

I came to Metro 31 years ago, which was three years after Richard did. However, I didn't really get to know Richard until about six years later. I never could have imagined how the next 25 years were going to play out. When I look back at all the accomplishments that took place, some that were crucial to our long-term survival, I realize how hard it is to pick just a few to talk about tonight.

In 1982 when Richard took what was considered to be a significant risk buying the Old Dominion Drydock, within just a few years two of our competitors (Jonathan Corporation and Horn Brothers) that chose not to expand to drydocking capability went out of business. While this was happening, Metro's workload and capability was continuing to increase while the industry was shrinking.

In 1993 Richard took what was considered again to be a significant risk; expanding into Chester, Pennsylvania in support of the Navy's need to maintain the AOE Class ships that were stationed at Earle Weapons Station in Colts Neck, New Jersey. Although we didn't make a lot of profit while we were there, we did maintain many jobs here in Norfolk for our existing workforce at the time when the local industry would not have been able to. The incredible demand that this put on the organization made numerous people step up in both locations to levels that were beyond even their own belief. I'm also convinced that this effort is what facilitated the ability for Metro to upgrade to Speede, our current drydock. These are just two of the many examples where Richard's vision and leadership navigated the company through dangerous times; taking well planned calculated risk while others chose to unknowingly take the larger risk of staying the course.

In 1987 when Richard first announced the ESOP to the workforce, the reaction was lukewarm at best. I think that many people were more suspicious than excited. I can't tell you how Richard was feeling at the time, but I can tell you that while we have worked together over the years, Richard was always committed to do what was best for the long- term interest of the employee owners, even when the result was perceived by some as doing something to them instead of something for them. He never wavered even when only we really understood why the action was for the benefit of the employees.

As you all know now, Richard's latest and certainly one of the most significant accomplishments was the sale of Metro to General Dynamics. It was quite a pleasure to see Richard go head to head with one of the industry's giants and not only hold his own but even back them down at times. Richard would never be bullied by anyone, and I can say that the building trades unions in Pennsylvania along with our neighbors BAE have certainly tried, but did not succeed.

In the case of the building trades in Chester, we were approximately 80% through the facility upgrades needed to accommodate the first ship when they intervened and insisted on a meeting with Metro when they found out we were using some non-union contractors. We agreed to meet them in a conference room at one of the local hotels. When they finally finished entering the room, the 19th and last union representative turned and locked the door. Their leader then started the meeting by saying, "We don't want to have to screw with you but we will if we have to." (He didn't actually use the word screw; I changed it since I felt this was a PG crowd.) Richard patiently waited for him to finish his speech without interruption, and then it was his turn. Shortly into Richard's comments, their leader, trying to play the tough guy, abruptly interrupted Richard. Then Richard proceeded to back him down in a way that left the other 18 people in total disbelief. At the end of the meeting the union reps were exchanging business cards with us, satisfied that they would be considered for future work. If that had not happened, we would not have been ready to execute the contract on time and would probably have lost it.

Another example is from the earlier and more combative days with BAE. I went with Richard to a meeting with Bill Clifford and Al Krechage. My counterpart Bill Clifford is about 5 feet 9 inches and Richard's was a former college football player. (This part becomes more relevant later in the story.) Shortly into the discussion, the meeting became so intense I began wondering to myself just how combative is this going to get. Then I thought I can take out Clifford if need be, but I'm not so sure Richard and I both can take out Al. We made it through the meeting, it never came to blows and when the negotiations were over, Metro prevailed again. This meeting was of such importance that had we lost, we might all be speaking with a British accent today. (No offense George.)

As tough as Richard can be when needed, he also has a heart of gold and a great deal of compassion for people. Like many of us throughout the years I had my share of challenges both at work and in my personal life. Richard was always there with heartfelt concern along with whatever support and guidance was needed. He was always able to bring some level of comfort to even the most serious situations.

I took great pleasure in seeing the reaction of the employees when the General Dynamics deal was announced. I also enjoyed hearing the many positive comments about Richard regarding the way he had always taken care of the employees. There were no lukewarm reactions out there this time. I feel so fortunate to have been given the opportunity to work so closely with Richard over the years. Richard has done so much for all of us that I feel like anything I say couldn't possibly be an adequate expression of how I feel. You have provided numerous opportunities for people over the years, and have changed so many lives. Richard, thank you for your guidance and friendship. I love you".

6: Tales of Rod

To Rich: December 23, 2010
From Lori Douglas (Wife of Rod)

Dear Mr. Goldbach,

"I would like you to accept this gift as a Christmas present considering it was originally purchased for you as an anniversary gift. I purchased this and was told that you had asked that no one give anything at all. I hope that maybe you can enjoy this gift on New Year's with Janet while we are celebrating our 16th anniversary!

I would like to take a few moments of your time and tell you my thoughts of certain recent events. First, I would like to explain that I recognize that there are few people in their lifetime that ever work in the field that they really truly love and, at the same time, are extremely talented and gifted to accomplish what you have. I have the utmost respect for your dedication to this company and realize that your dedication and foresight has brought this company to its current condition. I also know that you realize that you couldn't have done this alone! There are many people in this company that I admire because they have and are still dedicating many hours and years of their lives that also contributes to the success of this company. I don't know of any other company that has as many employees of more than 15 years as Metro. I think that alone says a lot!

This brings me to Rod. I have always known that he has a unique ability to see the beyond. To organize in his mind on many things at once at a difficult level and remember details from years ago. Although, I can ask him to meet me at Lonestar for the tenth time and he can't remember where it is. (Don't ask me!) I knew that one day he would be at a level of his career that he could only dream of. This company is his heart and soul. It's what he eats and breathes just as you do. His phone is constantly where we are and that's okay, because that's who he is. His dedication has given me a life that I could also never dream of which brings me to the point of this letter. The day that he was notified of the value of his bonuses, we sat on the pier in disbelief. We sat in silence with mixed emotions, excitement, scared, happy and guilty. Our lives had changed in many ways in minutes. He is at the top of his game and most of the country is falling apart. It's mind boggling! When the country was doing the best, this company was about to close the doors. Now that the country is at its worst the company has reached a level beyond comparison to any other in its category. I want you to know that we cannot thank you enough! There are no words to express our feelings and please know that it is greatly appreciated. Most of all, I want you to know that we believe in "paying it forward". We are helping many members of our families in ways that we have never been able to do before. We are very family oriented people and will do whatever it takes to take care of them. It has been a very long year with my mother's illness which I can't believe I can now say she is doing wonderful! Miracles do happen and I'm living it! I do want you to know that I think the most important thing to Rod is not the monetary value but that you have realized his dedication and ability which he often questions.

There is a saying that I recently put in my mother's room:

"Life is Not Waiting for the Storm to Pass, its Learning to Dance in the Rain!"

I think this is one of the most powerful statements I have ever heard. Metro's journey is a symbol of this saying.

Merry Christmas and Happy New Year!
Lori Douglas

7: *Tales of Beulah*

From Beulah F. Dawson to Rich September 28, 2011
To: My Boss, Mentor, Confidant and Best Good Friend
Richard A. Goldbach

Dear Mr. G.:

I want to start out by saying "congratulations on your retirement".

You are so amazing. Words cannot convey the love that you have disbursed to me during my 34 year stay here at Metro Machine. I love you just because. I've also learned that Love is not Love until you give it away, and that is exactly what you have done through the years. The love that we share is called agape love, Christian love. I thank God for you and you are so special to me.

In the beginning when I started working at Metro, I noticed that you had an open-door policy. That was the first thing that really impressed me about you. Employees were allowed to sit down and talk to the President.

My mind wanders back on the blessings that you have bestowed upon me: Just to name a few:

1. *In 1977 I was 19 years old and blessed to get a job here at Metro Machine with a high school diploma only.*

2. *In 1978, I had my first child Daphanie. I couldn't afford to pay my co-pays for the insurance, you allowed me to pay Metro Machine $10 a week until the balance was paid back.*

3. *You allowed Nenita Moreno to continuously advance me loans to then pay them back at $25 per week.*

4. *My husband was abusive, I missed work, and you never threatened to terminate me.*

5. *You also told me if I wanted to have my husband put away for years, you could do so because what he had done to me was against the law.*

6. *You gave me a pep talk about my son Ervin growing up and how you didn't want him to fall into his father's shoes. Ervin is now working at BAE as an electrician. He's a gospel rapper and has recorded a CD entitled Heaven Bound. You also allowed me to bring my children to work with me on Saturdays, I now have 4 grandchildren.*

7. *One particular payday, the bank had made some type of mistake with the check numbers, the employees could not get paid that Friday. You didn't ask us to wait until next week, Mr. G you hired a Brinks Armored truck along with two armed guards to come here and you paid us in cash. Your heart was for the employees.*

8. *You gave me and my family a shot at the cleaning contract here at Metro, the contract started off paying $740.00 per month and ended up paying nearly $3,000.00 per month.*

9. *My husband and I always drove ragged cars. One day I needed my pay check cashed so that I could get the car out of the shop. Janice & Jennifer took my check to the bank for me. The bank would not cash the check. Janice & Jennifer spotted you in the bank elevator with your guest and tried to explain what they needed. Your exact words were "these are my employees, you all go ahead, I will join you shortly". You then went into the bank with them and told the manager "these are my employees, give them whatever they want."*

10. *I stayed depressed and fat from having so many personal problems until I asked you if you could help me with a diet plan. The insurance would pay for the therapy, but not pay for the milk shakes, but you Mr. Goldbach, gave me the money out of your pocket to do this and I remember the exact words you said "Get your self-esteem back".*

11. *My mother came to work for you and you hired my sister Angela in 1987.*

12. During the Christmas Holidays one year I took part in the Christmas parade and I watched you and Mrs. G. walk through the Berkley community handing out poinsettias to families.

13. I got the opportunity to work in Philadelphia with Kristen & Larry, earn my regular paycheck and received a per diem check. They invited me and my husband to their home for dinner. I was so pleased to meet your grandchildren.

14. My husband got saved in the year 2000 and remained drug and alcohol free for 5 years until his death.

15. When we christened Speede, I got the opportunity to be on the program with all the big wheels, you of course, Paul Reason, Mayor Fraim and others. What an honor.

16. Last but not least, I get to receive my ESOP money, keep my job, and I didn't have to put any money into the plan. Mr. G. again, I'm so grateful. You're the father that I never had. I will never forget those precious memories.

I often tell people everywhere I go how you bless others, such as the Boys Club, St. Helena, Campostella, Berkley Early Childhood Center. You have been an angel to me and I have never met anyone in my life with such character, integrity and wisdom. You're a man of valor.

Please stay in touch. Guess what Mr. G.?? I'm going to buy me a husband with my money LOL!!!

Thank you so much. May God ever bless and keep you. I love you to life. We've grown older together. If I can ever be of help to you and your family, please call me @ 757-XXX-XXXX.

Sincerely,

Beulah F. Dawson (AKA Chicken Bone Beulah)

8: Tale of Ida

Ida retired from the Navy and came to work in the office at Metro Machine during my early days there. Before PCs, since I never employed a secretary at Metro Machine, I borrowed her frequently for typing services because I knew her to be responsive and reliable. Ida would come in to help me at any time, as long as she could bring her young daughter Becky into work with her.

After Ida was diagnosed with stomach cancer, she would come into my office periodically to discuss her thoughts as a dying mom. I spoke with her for hours as I held her hand in the hospital the day her cancer was to take her life. I believe Ida was in her upper thirties when she died.

All of us in the office went to her graveside funeral when she was buried several days later. I noticed Becky was not at the funeral, which I thought strange since they were inseparable.

After completing his remarks to the gathering, the minister said, "Mr. Goldbach, the others said you were the best one to speak for them. Would you be willing to say a few words on behalf of Ida?"

I had never done anything like that and was caught by surprise. I did the best I could.

Becky was brought to my office when she came to Metro Machine about ten years later, hoping to learn more about her Mom. I received this letter from her several days later:

"Mr. Goldbach,

Hello! How are you? It's Becky! I just wanted to thank you for being so nice to me last Thurs. I appreciate it beyond belief! You taking the time to share with me, your memories about my Mom meant the World to me. I always wondered who did Mom's eulogy. I guess I always assumed Daddy did it.

That was so nice of you and thanks for being there for my Mom when she turned to you and then for me when I did too. You are a wonderful man, Mr. Goldbach. I owe you one and I miss her so much, but now I had more than I had last week before I came to see ya'll. Thanks so much for her personnel file too. Now I have something of hers that my dad will never be able to get a hold of. Thanks to you!

Please thank Mike for the pictures also and tell Clyde thanks for talking to me about her. And everybody else too.

Thursday, Dec. 9 was a very special day that I'll never forget! Thanks to you and Mr. Newman! I know my Mom would be so proud to have worked with such wonderful people that were there for her then and are here for me now!

Ya know, Mr. Goldbach I'm so scared when I think about all the things she'll never be there to see, like my wedding, her grandchildren being born and to help me with my medical problems, but at least I have memories to feel closer to her!

Ya Know? Thanks again! Take care!
Eternally Grateful, K.I.T.
Becky "Ida's Loving Daughter

9: Tales of Metro Machine Shipwrights

Portrait by Janet Goldbach of Metro Machine Employee Owner, David Golt *(on right), with his beloved brother Freddie.*

Shipwrights are rugged individualists. There are no two the same. They are all interesting. You want every one of them on your side. You don't have to ask to find out what they are thinking. Trying to pick one to represent all of them is impossible. You take your life in your hands if you dare.

David is a typical shipyard worker. If you knew David and if you were looking for one person on Earth to trust with your life, you could do no better than him. Fiercely loyal to his wife Dev, his ten children and his siblings, he lets almost no one into his private world. Janet and I got a small peek once. We were most impressed with what we saw.

When ship repair work was slow one day, I hired Dave to drive Janet from Pennsylvania to Norfolk. As they were driving through a rural part of Delaware, Janet remembered David had lived somewhere around there and so she asked him if he wanted to drive past his old home. David replied that he would and, after thinking about it, told Janet he had two brothers living in Delaware almost directly along the planned route. He said he would like to show her something up in their attic, something that he felt was quite unique.

Only brother Freddie was home, so the three of them walked upstairs to the attic. What David and Freddie showed Janet was a part of the old Underground Railway located under the roof eves. How agonizing it must have been for those who had to cower there, nose to toes.

After they went back outside, the artist in Janet was struck by how interesting and quite wonderful the faces of the two brothers were. She asked if she could take a picture of them together. That's how Dave became my typical shipyard worker!

Both were agreeable but stood about seven feet apart. Asking if they would please stand closer, David moved about six inches. With continuing encouragement from Janet, David, bit by bit, moved closer to Freddie until Freddie finally said, "It's only for a picture" and they put their arms around each other. Hoping she had her masterpiece, Janet quickly snapped a picture. That was the only photo she had time to take before the brothers separated.

Janet was finishing the painting months later in her studio in the Arts Center @319 in Smithfield. As she was, one of David's sons, who was working there in Smithfield, was shocked to suddenly see his Dad as he was passing by the studio where Janet painted. Of course, he told his father about it. David, taken completely by surprise, came to see it. Unfortunately, Janet wasn't there that day.

At Janet's invitation, David and Dev came to view the painting in Janet's home studio. That evening and again the next day, David called Freddie to tell him the good news about the portrait of the two of them with their arms around each other. Sadly, it was too late. Freddie had died during the night.

Janet believes that it's possible her "masterpiece" may be the only portrayal of the affection that the two brothers really had for each other.

Naval ship repair placed extraordinary demands on the Metro Machine shipwrights as each did their daily share of the Company's collective effort. Every day presented a work task different from every other day. Every day presented a work site different from every other day. Every day, each shipwright would perform a work task different from every other shipwright. The safety and success of every shipwright was dependent on every other shipwright always performing their own work task in a safe and competent way. If ever there was a band of brothers and sisters, it was the shipwrights of Metro Machine, whether each happened to like every one of the others every day or not. That is the world David and his fellow employee owners lived in and prospered in at Metro Machine. I was thrilled every day of the 34 years of my Metro Machine life they let me live in that world with them.

10: Tales of Coach

Metro Machine, starting in about 1983, became the largest and most prominent sponsor of the Southside Boys and Girls Club, which serves the youth of the Berkley neighborhood of Norfolk, Virginia. Metro Machine has always been located in Berkley and many of Metro Machine's workers have always resided there.

For many of the kids who would grow up in Berkley and later work at Metro Machine as adults, Southside was the only positive social presence in their lives. With the guidance I received from Coach Elwood Williams, Executive Director of Southside Boys and Girls Club, I came to realize that the long-term interests of Southside were indistinguishable from the long-term interests of Metro Machine.

Accordingly, the organization of Metro Machine became indistinguishable from the organization of Southside Boys Club in 1983 and stayed that way until 2011, when the Metro stock owned by its employees was sold to a large public corporation.

I was very surprised but thrilled to be named the 1990 Layman of the Year for outstanding leadership and support of the Virginia/DC Area Council Boys and Girls Clubs of America.

In 2007, Coach asked me to give the keynote talk at the annual

fundraising banquet organized by Kenny Newman. Kenny, Executive V.P. of Metro Machine, took over as President of Southside Boys and Girls Club when I needed to resign the post after fifteen years.

This is what I said:

"Each of us is here tonight because, one way or another, we have come to support the efforts of Coach Williams. To meet Coach, I, first, had to find my way from Mobile to Norfolk. That happened in 1977 when I was fired from my job at Ingalls shipbuilding and Norfolk's Metro Machine turned out to be the only place I could get work.

The buildings I drove past in Metro's Berkley neighborhood were more run-down than in any place I had ever spent any time. My response to that, at the time, was making sure I never slowed my car down between Metro and the Berkley Bridge.

A 1977 Virginian Pilot article, that mentioned Berkley, happened to catch my eye. It was about a man who had managed to raise the money to build a new boy's club there.

My daughter, Kristen, had to play a soprano saxophone as part of her speech therapy. She hated it. I don't know if you've ever heard a soprano saxophone played by a teenager who hates it, but take it from me, you don't want to be around. As soon as I could, I got the saxophone out of the house.

The only one I knew of that might help me do that was this Boy's Club guy, so I had one of our workers take it out to him. I used this approach so I could take a tax deduction, even though the saxophone had been given to me. Meanwhile, Janet renewed her business of entertaining adults and kids with the magic she had started performing on New York TV in 1947.

I warned her that there were certain unsafe Norfolk neighborhoods, like Berkley, that she needed to avoid. She ignored my advice and carried her magic apparatus in her Oldsmobile station wagon to any place that would book her for a performance. One day in 1981, two ODU students booked her for a kid's show over near Metro. They did it solely for the purpose of getting extra credit for a course they were taking. I told Janet the place they wanted her to go wasn't safe and she shouldn't do it. When she persisted, I insisted on joining her.

You can imagine what a threatening sight a white woman in a pixie costume and a white man in a suit and tie made on the streets of Berkley in 1981. As Janet proceeded to set up her apparatus inside a building on the corner of Berkley and South Main, a man approached me.

He introduced himself as "Coach". I recalled the name from the article and told him that I was the generous guy that had sent him the soprano saxophone. We got into a conversation that lasted through the show, much to Janet's frustration, since it distracted the kids. When the show was over, while I didn't know it at the time, I had just met a man that would change many lives during the next 28 years, including mine.

When I decided to buy Janet a new station wagon a few months later, I decided to save money by selling the Oldsmobile, instead of trading it. In two weeks, I had only one man come to look at it. He started discussions by pointing out everything that was wrong with the car. I replied that, if he felt that way, why didn't he get out of my yard. I stomped into the house and he drove off.

He called back in an hour and said he would pay my asking price. I responded that he was a jerk and I would give the car away before selling it to him at any price. He said that was illegal and that he was going to the police. I hung up on him but started to worry that he would really do what he said. Thinking that I needed to quickly dump the car, I called the "Coach" guy I had met, and told him he could have the car but only if he picked it up, right away.

Coach showed up a couple of hours later and drove off in the evidence. The police never did show up. A week later, presumably because of my apparent generosity, I was invited to attend a Boys Club board meeting. In that meeting, a fight almost broke out between black and white board members to settle different opinions about school busing to achieve racial balance, a really hot topic at the time. I felt right at home.

Boys Club board meetings were just like Metro's progress meetings with the Navy and just like the discussions I had with my teenage kids. I signed up and became a regular attendee. Coach pulled me aside six months later and told me the Oldsmobile's GM diesel engine had stopped working and the cost of fixing it was higher than the cost of replacing the car. It turned out that the car buyer I was trying to one-up, had been right all along. But it was too late. Coach had found his way under my skin and he was destined to stay there.

Since I was fresh out of personal cars to give away we turned to recycling Metro's Ford Taurus station wagons through Coach. Such was the start of a beautiful relationship that has been an essential part of the company's existence.

After 25 years of being under Coach's spell; support of his love, respect and concern for the kids of Berkley has made Coach's quest, the quest of all of us that work at Metro Machine. As I watch Coach plotting and scheming on a night such as this, as he works the room with the talent of Bill Clinton, for the benefit of his kids, I am reminded of the day he found me in Berkley. I watch Coach at the club, flinching every time he sees one of his kids do something he knows will disappoint himself. I see his look of relief every time he sees a kid experience even the smallest success. I watch him as he uses calm and quiet words to redirect, console and encourage kids, when they need it. It seems his lips hardly move.

But the kids hear what he says. They listen, nod and charge off in a new direction. I see him using his gentle touch to impart his own courage into the hearts of youngsters to overcome their fear and dread. As, little by little, Coach and his staff enter the souls of these kids; I see pride, self-reliance and inspiration gradually displace the negative emotions the kids bring through the doors of the club, when they enter.

But, it isn't enough to feel those things inside the security of the club, because life as an adult is, inevitably, outside, where the only security is the person you have become. Every day they walk out those same doors, the kids are a tiny bit more prepared and a tiny bit more inspired to reckon with the evil and inhumane street forces they must confront alone. More and more of those kids, when they walk out those doors to adulthood, are determined to follow a path that leads to the university and fulfillment instead of a path to the penitentiary and empty existence.

Some of those that have found it within themselves to accomplish this are among us tonight. We honor them as we honor Coach and his staff. As I hope you can tell from my words, Coach resides in me, full time, now. Janet wants you know that he lives inside her, as well. As each of you thinks about why you are here tonight, you will find it is because Coach's spirit also lives inside of you.

The chain of events that I have described that caused that to happen to me isn't what you might have expected or what I might have preferred to relate to you. But, Coach capitalized on what did happen, so what does it matter. The kids don't care. What matters is that all of us here have been brought to the kids of Berkley by this single unremarkable but determined man, who has dedicated his every waking thought and deed to those same kids for 35 years.

Please join me in showing our love and respect for Coach and assuring him that, by our presence tonight, we are renewing our vows to support his life's work."

11: Tale of Gerri

From Gerri to Rich August7, 1997

Mr. Goldbach,

I just wanted to take this opportunity to let you know how grateful I am for all that you have done for me. I know that I could not have attended Virginia Tech had it not been for the scholarship you so generously provided me. I realize that I do not say it often enough, but please know that not a day goes without my thanking the heavens above for your selflessness, your generosity, and especially your patience. I know that I struggled through some semesters, but your faith in me has enabled me to endure.

I understand that you are an extremely busy individual, but I would greatly appreciate the opportunity to thank you in person. While I do not come home to Tidewater often, I will make whatever arrangements necessary to guarantee that this meeting takes place. Please have Antoinette notify me of your availability.

I will be graduating on Saturday, May 9, 1998 and would be honored if you would attend. There is also a smaller graduation ceremony, held by one of my own organizations, on the eve of the commencement. I would be honored if you could attend this ceremony as well. I would really like for you to get a better feel for the impact I have been able to have on this university, especially since it was you that provided me with the chance to attend this fine institution.

Thank you again for everything. While I can never truly repay you, I hope that I will continue to make you proud.

Sincerely,
Gerri

From Rich to Gerri – no date but in response to preceding letter

Dear Gerri,

I have had your letter of last August in my desk since receiving it, al-

ways hoping our meeting would take place soon. That meeting will occur, if not before your graduation, in Blacksburg, at your graduation...where both my wife and I will attend.

My interest in you and your life is extraordinary. The day will come when you know that from direct contact. For now, this letter will have to suffice.

From the day, I first met Coach Williams, I wanted to play some kind of important role in his life's work. The "Better Me" program was the idea that came to me to achieve that goal although the name for the program came from Coach. My dream was to have a number of deserving Southside youth find enough incentive in the program to fight to overcome the personal obstacles that are beyond the reach of any program put together by outsiders. Even now, my own life's experience doesn't let me remotely conceive of the outside obstacles you know were enormous but that you survived through. This personal journey creates within me a strong feeling of respect and love for you. Now, wherever you go and whatever you do, your life will be part of the continuum of mine.

I want you to be aware that my affection for and concern for you was strongest at the time in our relationship which caused you the most resentment. That time when you slipped and I made you find your own way back. Right or wrong, I was convinced that helping you when the failure was your own would cause permanent harm to the self-sufficiency you were acquiring and would need throughout life. I hope you will come to regard that episode the way that I do – as a watershed stage of your life which will provide confidence in the future to draw upon inner resources you don't know are there – to confront the unpredictable crises still left for you and the despair they may cause.

I truly appreciate the kind words for me in your letter. Whatever life has given me to pass on to you came to me from fewer than ten others, one of whom never knew me. I believe that this passing on of an opportunity and hope is the gift of life. My fondest hope for you is that you come to know this gift by yourself enriching the lives of others.

Sincerely,
Richard Goldbach

From Gerri to Rich April 27, 1998

Dear Mr. Goldbach,

Words cannot express the emotions I felt when I received your card. I was overwhelmed by your kindness, but more so by your honesty and sincerity. I am flattered to know that you have so much faith in me, and that I continue to make you proud. I know that you did not have to go out on such a limb for me, but I am so very grateful that you did. I smile knowing that you, being a man I still have yet to meet have such a devoted interest in my wellbeing. I live each day thanking God for sending you my way. You are one of the many angels He has blessed me with, and for that I say thank you.

While I know that I could never repay you for all that you have done for me, please know that I hope to influence others as you have me. I hope to be a pillar of strength and hope for other youth. I want to be able to give the same opportunities to others that were given to me. I know that no one can make it in this world alone. The love and guidance I have received from individuals like Coach Williams and you prove that anything is possible. While I was not as troubled as some other youth you may have come in contact with, I was (am) not without my obstacles. Your role in my life has been critical in that you were an integral source of confidence, heart, and inspiration.

I want you to know that I cherish all that these five years at Virginia Tech have taught me; the good, the bad, and even the in-between. As you stated in your card, these experiences have allowed me to come into my own. They have strengthened my faith, my spirit, and my character. While the courage came from within, I thank you for your patience, faith and love.

Enclosed you will find invitations to my graduation ceremonies as earlier described. I look forward to the opportunity to meet both you and your wife. I apologize if this is late notice, but I also wanted to include information from the Who's Who recognition ceremony.

Also enclosed is a copy of my employment contract. I accepted a position as an Associate Consultant with PeopleSoft. I will be relocating to Pleasanton, CA. for training (about nine months) before relocating permanently to Atlanta, GA. My base salary is $39,000 for the first 18 months *(training and Associate Consultant status), however my earning potential while in training is $45,000 including bonuses. After training, I become an Associate Consultant and my income bracket can go as high as $68,000 (including bonuses). This bracket will continue to grow as I enter the ranks of full Consultant.*

I thank you for the opportunity to work for Metro Machine; however, employment with PeopleSoft is the chance of a lifetime. This is truly a phenomenal company with great benefits and booming business. I know that you have my best interest at heart, and will understand my decision. I just wanted to make sure you knew how much I appreciated the offer you extended to me.

Again, I thank you for everything. While this is the end of my academic tenure, it is the beginning of my career, and our friendship. I have every intention of keeping in touch with you, and hope that you are able to do the same.

Sincerely,
Gerri

12: Tales of La-Goldia

It is not reasonable to expect to successfully operate long term, a labor-intensive business that depends on local residents for its workforce, if the business and the neighborhood are not both successful. Metro Machine is located on the perimeter of the Berkley neighborhood, one of Norfolk's several very difficult "Inner City" neighborhoods. There are five or more businesses that call themselves shipyards that are located on the part of the Norfolk waterfront located in Berkley. Together with their subcontractors, they provide most of the manufacturing wage jobs in Berkley.

One day in the late 1990s, I received a telephone call from the Norfolk Police Chief. He asked me to join him and the Beacon Light Civic League headed by Mr. George Banks on a "Take Back the Streets" march. He wanted to hold it the next night through the most blighted streets in Berkley. I told him I would get back to him.

Except for my work on the Metro Machine premises and my visits to the Southside Boys Club, where I always parked closely, I had never gone out on foot in Berkley at night. So, before I agreed to take back the streets, I asked Coach Williams, my expert on Berkley, if he thought I'd be safe.

Coach said he would join me and as long as I was with him, the Police Chief and Mr. George Banks, I should be safe. I called the Police Chief and told him I would join him the next night. I suspected then, and do to this day, that the three of them had cooked up this drafting of me from the very beginning. But, I'll never ask and they would never tell, even if I did.

Just to be sure I was safe, though, I also called Bob Claffee, owner of Anchor Vending, and asked him to set up a dinner picnic for 200 Metro Machine and subcontractor worker/marchers on one of the Metro Machine piers the next night. To eat, you first had to march.

The planned march and dinner became the talk at work the next day. Shipyard workers are a curious and adventurous lot, usually ready for any new experience. I had 200 enthusiastic reinforcements ready to join me on the march.

We certainly had our share of jeers along the march route. But,

I was certain I saw hope in the eyes of many of the spectators who watched quietly. Those boarded up buildings and crumbled streets surely looked different at sunset on foot that day than they had on prior occasions when I had driven quickly through them in daylight hours in the safety of my car.

As we ate our picnic dinners back at the shipyard, Coach said he had a new idea. In his case this meant he had been thinking of it for years and was waiting for just the right moment. His idea was to put together an annual Christmas parade through the Berkley streets with Metro Machine providing the "anchor" float and Coach putting everything else together including the bands. "Sounds good to me", I told him and turned over float design and construction to Joe Eckel, Metro Machine Maintenance Foreman.

Joe's Christmas float design turned out to be the Metro flatbed truck decorated for Christmas, Metro Machine workers dressed as Santa's elves and hundreds of poinsettias. Joe said, "I'd like you and Janet to walk behind the float so you can carry the poinsettias to the grandmothers sitting on the porches as the Metro elves hand them to you. This concept worked nicely for several Christmases. But then the "grandmother" secret got out. When it did, many of the standing spectators tried to negotiate their way into grandmother status, including teen-age girls and guys.

I would rather negotiate with the Navy any day. Janet thought it was a lark and did her negotiating with her beautiful smile. Guess who was the best negotiator that day.

At the end parade stop, there were still poinsettias left. We were rushed by a crowd of "grandmothers". I fought for truth and justice. Janet smiled and teased. Neither approach worked, but at least we didn't have to carry any poinsettias back to the Metro Machine shipyard, as we had after previous parades.

I was weary as I climbed into the bus that was to take us back to the shipyard from the parade ending point. Everyone else climbed in – except one. Janet was missing! I walked back to look out the rear window and there she was – still outside jabbering with a magician's kindred soul, a lady dressed in a clown suit for the parade.

I rapped on the window and beckoned. Janet glanced up and

gave me her very sweetest "You're invisible" look and returned to her conversation. I stomped off the bus.

As I walked up, Janet said, "This is La-Goldia Williamson, librarian at St. Helena's Elementary School and she doesn't have any books. I'm going to give her some."

With this, La-Goldia turned on me. She said, "Oh, Mr. Goldbach, please come and visit my library. I'll buy your lunch."

I replied, "Why in the world would I want to visit a library that doesn't have any books?" She said, "That's why I want you to come. I want to show you our new "Accelerated Reader Program." I agreed to come over one day as soon as she returned after Christmas.

I found St. Helena's Elementary School, which I discovered had been less than one mile from my office for all those years without my knowing it. La-Goldia fussed about my lunch apparently so she could get it out of the way to get on with her real agenda. After an undue amount of effort, she produced a cup of colored water she had the nerve to call "punch" and a still-frozen tuna fish sandwich (without lettuce).

I said, "Aren't you going to join me?" She replied that she never ate lunch. I said, "I wouldn't either if it looked, felt and tasted like this." She smiled a most beautiful smile. I knew then that she was going to get whatever she wanted and more. It was just a matter of time.

Diane Williams, instructional specialist, joined us next, clutching a large clump of wooden pencils emblazoned with "Accelerated Reader Program". She said she didn't eat lunch either, which gave me an excuse to end that painful part of the agenda. She said proudly, "We give the children one of these pencils if they read an approved book and can answer the questions on the monitor. What do you think?"

I replied, "I wouldn't read one sentence for one of those pencils, with or without answering questions." Looking at the nearly empty bookshelves around us, I added, "Not that you have to worry about it since you don't have any books, anyway." La Goldia said, "The children take the books home and don't bring them back." I said, "I can fix that."

Diane said, "We don't have nearly enough monitors, there is no one to fix the ones we have, we don't have the software we need, the software we have doesn't work, we don't have the cabling we need or anyone to install it, we don't have the printers we need."

I said, "Anything else?" Diane said, "We don't know."

I said, "I can fix all of that, including what you don't know. And as long as I don't have to finish that sandwich, I'll have a proposal in the hands of your Principal right after New Year's. It won't cost you a cent. These kids will have what they need."

And, indeed they did for the next 12 years until I sold Metro Machine to General Dynamics on behalf of its employee-owners.

I went back that December 1997 day and told managing employee-owners that the Berkley kids' reading problem is Metro Machine's problem because we need our future workers to be able to read. With Metro Machine employee-owner reading support costing Metro Machine less than 300 thousand dollars each year, St. Helena's went from near the bottom of Norfolk schools in reading and writing each year to near the top. What an inconsequential price to pay for such a result!

The Metro Machine employee-owners would make sure the St. Helena's/Metro Machine Float, with its cargo of top St. Helena's fully-costumed codebreaker readers, would be selected as best in the important Downtown Norfolk annual Christmas Parade virtually every year. Even when they came in second some years, the kids and everybody watching knew they really were the best.

A surprising number of $1000 college scholarships were awarded in accordance with the terms of the proposal. One young man was awarded a total of $4000 and was presented a scholarship by Norfolk Academy. Norfolk Academy is one of the top private schools in the nation.

Metro Machine made sure that every kid had a laptop and every classroom had one of those amazing electronic learning tables, whatever they're called. We came to trust St. Helena's professionals Whatever they thought could help the kids, if we had a little spare money that week, they got it.

Ten or so years later, I was facing hundreds of bright faced well dressed, happy and polite kids who had come to receive their annual reading awards in the Nauticus Theater in the proud presence of beloved teachers and parents. I had been asked to say a few words.

The few words I planned to say were that I had come to be convinced that the Police Chief and I had never been the ones to take back the streets of Berkley. The kids in front of me were the only ones who could take back the streets. But, they had to read to do it!

Horribly, I couldn't get the words out. They were just too important!

I just stood in front of all those kids and cried. The kids were bewildered. I was acutely embarrassed. Finally, a few parents, realizing what had happened, got the audience to clap until I was able to stop.

I never was able to get the words out, until I managed to write this short passage, over eight years later. Even then, it took a long, long time.

The program was named the "Codebreaker Program" consistent with the conclusion of a most remarkable Harlem woman with a name I have forgotten whom I happened to see on Public Broadcasting that same first Christmas season. She said, "Reading is the code for all learning. If you don't break that code by the fifth grade, you are finished learning for life."

Lillian Thomas is the courageous Principal who trusted that a shipyard CEO and his employees whom she had never met, would do what they promised to do for her kids.

Very sadly, sweet and lovely La-Goldia, whose clown costume, persistence and smile triggered it all, died before she could see the wonders her life had brought to the World.

La-Goldia smiled down on me one day at Nauticus after one of the annual Accelerated Reader Award Ceremonies.

A gentleman I didn't know pulled me aside and said, "I need to talk to you. Thank you for teaching my son how to read." I replied that I was pleased that he was proud of his son and that he came to Nauticus to see him get his award.

Then he said, "That is not what I came over to tell you. What I want to tell you is that, **My son is teaching me how to read!**"

I know I will take those words to my own ending. Thank you La-Goldia.

Unfortunately, Wall Street EBITDA expectations for the buyer of the stock owned by Metro Machine employee-owners led the new owner to terminate the Code Breaker Program. Camelot left St. Helena's on November 1, 2011.

If Wall Street would give consideration to the kids that are the future of America in its performance expectations, there would be fewer streets to take back. If it does not, I believe Corporate America may find itself trying to take Wall Street back.

Metro Machine Reading Program Offer made by Richard Goldbach on July 7, 1998 and accepted by St. Helena's Elementary School Principal Lillian Thomas:

Subject Program is proposed for your comments:

Purpose:

1. *Motivate students at all grade levels to achieve higher levels of literacy and to place greater importance on intellectual accomplishment.*

2. *Provide special recognition for teachers who achieve the highest levels of student literacy improvement.*

3. *Provide funding for additional school library books as student reading expands.*

4. *Impose discipline over return of books by students.*

Student Award Program

This program will be structured to provide personalized awards to students over a six-year period (K-5 Grade) at major reading milestone levels with intermediate awards between milestones which are not personalized. No major milestone awards will be made to students until all previously borrowed books are returned or paid for. Books delinquent at program start will be forgiven.

The program will be devised to induce students to "Break the Code" to education by learning to enjoy reading and by becoming literate. As students participate in the program they will advance through progressive "code breaker" ranks patterned after the Navy. Each of these ranks will have a body of books available to read appropriate to the rank which qual-

ifies for earning points toward the next rank. Each rank will entitle the student to the personalized uniform of that rank. i.e.

Midshipman Code breaker – Bookmark with ten (10) intermediate stickers.

Ensign Code breaker – Cap with ten (10) intermediate pins.

Lieutenant Code breaker – Back pack with ten (10) intermediate patches.

Commander Code breaker – Long sleeve sport shirt with ten (10) intermediate cloth badges.

Captain Code breaker – Varsity sweater with eleven (11) intermediate letters (CODE BREAKER)

Admiral Code breaker – Varsity jacket with intermediate sleeve stripes/stars

All uniforms will be in school colors emblazoned with the school logo. Students will earn uniform items up through Captain rank as they accumulate points under the accelerated reading program calibrated to national reading achievement levels. The goal of the program will be that:

- *Bookmarks will be awarded when students read at the end of Kindergarten level. Students must thereafter read 1st grade books.*
- *Caps will be awarded when students read at the end of 1st grade level. Students must thereafter read 2nd grade books.*
- *Back packs will be awarded when students read at the end of 2nd grade level. Students must thereafter read 3rd grade books.*
- *Sport shirts will be awarded when students read at the end of 3rd grade level. Students must thereafter read 4th grade books.*
- *Sweaters will be awarded when students read at the end of 4th grade level. Students must thereafter read 5th grade books.*
- *One star admiral jackets will be awarded when students read at the end of 5th grade level. Students must thereafter read 6th grade books.*
- *Two-star admiral rank will be awarded when students read at*

the end of 6th grade level together with a $1,000 scholarship deposit. Students must thereafter read 7th grade books.

- *Three-star admiral rank will be awarded when students read at the end of 7th grade level together with a second $1,000 scholarship deposit. Students must thereafter read 8th grade books.*
- *Four-star admiral rank will be awarded when students read at the end of 8th grade level together with a third $1,000 scholarship deposit.*
- *Special education students will be appropriately appraised and awards made based on this appraisal.*
- *The sole determinant of qualification for all Admiral ranks will be scores based on state or national standardized test formally administered by the Norfolk School System.*

Awards, which are outgrown or worn out, will be replaced at no cost when old item is turned in satisfactorily.

All students should be given a standardized test at the start of the program or when they enter the program through transfer to determine their reading grade level and the rank at which they start the program.

All students must read books at or above their rank in order to score points. No points will be awarded for student retests of individual books.

Teacher Award Program

This program will be structured to provide Certificate of Accomplishment and Cash Awards to teachers whose students earn the most points under the Accelerated Reading Program each year.

The top 20% will receive Certificates of Cum Laude Accomplishment and $100 cash awards.

The top 10% will receive Certificates of Magna Cum Laude Accomplishment and $250 cash awards.

The top teacher will receive a Certificate of Summa Cum Laude Accomplishment and a $1,000 cash award.

All student and teacher awards will be furnished by Metro Machine to St. Helena's based on data to be regularly supplied to Metro Machine which is subject to audit. Awards will be made by St. Helena's.

Students will be issued uniform awards by their teachers in the classroom as these awards are earned. Certificates for students and teachers will be conveyed at an annual award ceremony to be held at Nauticus Theater at the end of each school year. Cash awards to teachers will also be made at this ceremony. All students and teachers being granted certificates and their families will be given free attendance to Nauticus and a free Nauticus meal voucher. Costs of this award ceremony will be paid by Metro Machine.

Metro Machine will also sponsor a St. Helena's Elementary School Code Breaker Scholar float in each City of Norfolk Christmas Festival of Lights Parade. The Summa Cum Laude teacher and top reader in each classroom will represent St. Helena's on this float.

Metro Machine will supplement City Technical staff.

Finally, Metro Machine will contribute one dollar ($1.00) to the St. Helena's library book fund for each point earned by each student under the Accelerated Reading Program. This contribution will be made monthly. Metro Machine will also provide a single St. Helena's Code Breaker Scholar Flag which will be posted each month outside the classroom which accumulates the most points.

Your comments on this proposal will be appreciated. We look forward to implementing this program as soon as possible to support your worthy efforts in this area.

Very truly yours,
METRO MACHINE CORPORATION
Richard A. Goldbach
President

The following Proposal to Receive Funds for the Accelerated reader program at St. Helena Elementary School December 9, 1998 was submitted to Metro Machine President Richard Goldbach and accepted by him:

"Purpose: To increase the reading levels of students and to provide recognition and awards for successful reading.

Objective: Students will have access to classroom sets of Accelerated Reader books to read and test on. Awards and recognition will be given to those students attaining 5 or more points in grade 2-3; 10 or more in grade

4-5. The students will be recognized and awarded on the morning news show once each month.

Materials needed:

Item

Classroom sets of Accelerated Reader Titles

Awards & Incentives

(approximately 100 per month for 5 months)

Total Amount Needed

Students will continue to read, check out, and test on Accelerated reader books. Classroom teachers will monitor student's performance and keep track of points earned by students. On the first Wednesday of each month, the Instructional Specialist will collect points earned by students from each teacher. Students will receive awards and recognition the following Friday on the St. Helena News Show.

The first Friday of every month will be Accelerated Reading Awards Day on the morning news show.

The classroom teachers, instructional specialist and media specialist will all work together to implement the program.

Evaluation

Students Accelerated Reading Records will determine success of the program. Standardized tests will also be viewed to check improvements in reading; vocabulary and comprehension.

Accelerated Reader Team: Lillian Thomas, Principal, Diane Williams, Instructional Specialist and La-Goldia Williamson, Library Media Specialist and Susan Tardy, 5th Grade Classroom Teacher.

13: *Tales of Duck Church Pastor Bill*

Ruth, Janet's Mom, and Frank, Janet's Dad, came to live with us in Mobile, Alabama in 1971, when they were both 71. Ruth died in 1985 at the age of 85 and Frank died in 1989 on his half birthday. As Janet says, "He was 89 1/2 the day he died."

As my workplace issues continued to decline at Ingalls in the mid 1970s, Ruth's Cancer continued to progress and Frank had to contend with no longer having the stature his magic and title abstract work had provided throughout his life. Janet was the stalwart who held the six of us, including Kristen and Rick, together. We all also turned to Dauphin Way United Methodist Church in Mobile, one of the South's great churches. It became an increasingly important part of all of our lives. We all missed it greatly when my work brought us all to Norfolk.

As Ruth's health declined, it became harder and harder to seek out a replacement for Dauphin Way. Instead, Ruth turned to preachers on television she could reach out and touch on-screen.

Janet and I had been spending weekends after Ruth died in a new home on the ocean in Duck, NC. We had constructed it to bring our busy lives back together. Periodic attendance at Duck Church services was a part of that effort. We had recently added a Gazebo to our Duck house which became one of our most peaceful spots.

At the time, we were on the look-out for a fitting way to honor the lives of Ruth and Frank. After the church service one Sunday, Pastor Bill Ruth announced he had a schematic drawing for the placement of the new church building he was encouraging. I wanted to head for home but Janet wished to stay. I excused myself for a few minutes and when I returned, the short meeting was over. On the way home, Janet told me what was explained and mentioned two parallel lines drawn in the upper right hand corner of the plan. These lines were leading to an area where "someday a building, perhaps a social area for the teenagers" might be built.

I mentioned to Janet that the building might provide an opportunity for us to honor her Mom and Dad with a gazebo. Janet concurred. After the next church service, Janet and I advised the Chairman of the Building Committee of our desires and asked if Duck Church would consider a proposal from us to construct the building discussed the previous Sunday..

After he said the Committee would, I told him we would submit a proposal to design and build the gazebo, starting construction right away. This was the proposal I submitted:

To Frances R. Phillips (treasurer, Duck Church) dated March 5, 1990

Dear Mrs. Phillips:

This will confirm the pledge by my wife Janet and me to provide necessary funds to Duck United Methodist Church to enable the Church to construct on its property a general-purpose building to be named the "Francis and Ruth Clinton Memorial Hall". This building has previously been described as "the gazebo".

We commit to provide adequate funds to cover the ultimate cost, whatever it may be under the following conditions:

1. *The project will consist of a four-foot-wide walkway from the new church deck to Currituck Sound, a small open deck with benches on the sound and a 25-foot diameter building on high ground slightly east of the sound. The walkway will have small seating areas approximately every 50 to 75 feet and a stair entrance to a future picnic area on the high ground.*

2. *All work will be performed by Mr. Olin Finch as exclusively directed by me. Mr. Finch will keep the church building committee appraised of plans as they develop and/or change from time to time. The committee will have the opportunity to provide comments regarding the changes for my consideration but will not be authorized to provide direction to Mr. Finch on portions of the project funded by me. However, it is the intent of my wife and I to provide a building fully satisfactory to the building committee to the extent a building committee consensus exists and required funds are reasonable. The building itself will be reasonably consistent with drawings and verbal descriptions previously provided by Mr. Finch to the committee.*

3. *I enclose a $1,000 check for you to open a special Duck United Methodist Church checking account to be used for the exclusive purpose of paying for costs of this project. Costs of the project will be directly invoiced to Duck United Methodist Church via Mr. Finch. Mr. Finch and I will review and approve these invoices in writing before transmitting them to you. My wife and I will then contribute adequate funds to the church for you to deposit in the special account and make payments for the approved invoices. These funds are intended for the purpose of constructing this project and are to be only disbursed by you to pay invoices approved by me in writing. Payment of invoices must be within seven calendar days of receipt of funds from me in order to protect Mr. Finch's credit. Upon my request at any time, you will be required to provide a fully certified accounting of all deposits into and disbursements from the special account.*
4. *As we discussed, you will apply for sales tax rebates and deposit these rebates in the special account for use of paying project invoices.*
5. *In general, I expect completion of this project within 60 days and final payment of all invoices within 90 days.*

My wife and I are pleased to have the opportunity to make this gift to Duck United Methodist and look forward to working with you and all the others associated with the overall church expansion activities.

Very truly yours,
Richard A. Goldbach

The Architectural Committee accepted my proposal and we proceeded, completing the gazebo before the old church was removed. After the actual design of the Clinton Memorial Hall became apparent to Pastor Bill Ruth, he decided to change its name to the Clinton Memorial Walkway and Chapel in The Woods. He declared it should be open 24 hours per day, 365 days a year to any and all in need of a place for meditation and/or prayer.

The centerpiece of the Chapel is a beautiful stained glass window portraying important aspects of Ruth and Frank Clinton's lives including the famous saying by Stephen Grellet that Frank Clinton lived by every day of his life:

"I expect to pass through this world but once:
Any good thing, therefore, that I can do,
Or any kindness that I can show to any fellow creature,
Let me do it now.
Let me not defer or neglect it.
For I shall not pass this way again."

Kristen and Larry alongside the stained glass window in the Clinton Chapel, Duck Church, N.C.

With Pastor Bill Ruth's loving encouragement, the Church itself was completed in time for our daughter Kristen and her husband Larry Ehmer to be married in it on July 24, 1993.

Kristen, Bill Ruth, Father Tony, Larry; Duck Church Sanctuary, July 1993

Bill Ruth's love of music was on clear display in the original Duck Church as he played the piano and sang enthusiastically and beautifully facing the congregation. That love seemed the perfect place to memorialize my own parents, Charlotte and Frank Goldbach. We asked Bill to pick out the organ he most wanted to compliment his singing. Bill happily complied and sang with gusto each time he played his new organ in his new church.

Neither Mom nor Dad was to ever hear Bill play the Duck Church organ, although Bill did have one other opportunity to speak to Mom before she died.

Charlotte Goldbach (Mom) with Bill Ruth at Duck Church in 1993

Because Bill Ruth had brought Duck Church so completely into our lives, the Goldbach family was heartsick when it learned that Bill Ruth had to give up Duck Church to a pastor who had been preaching in the western end of North Carolina by the name of David Clift.

14: Tales of Duck Church Pastor David

After Bill Ruth sadly left Duck Church, Janet and I were eager to meet his successor, Pastor David Clift.

Janet and I, having missed David's first service because of traveling, spoke with one of our fellow parishioners and asked about David. We learned that Michael, one of David's two teen-age sons, had been killed in an automobile accident shortly before he departed for Duck. David's surviving son, Mark, was therefore the only son with David when he arrived in Duck.

We attended a church dinner scheduled for Saturday night to welcome David. There was an empty seat next to Janet. Empty seats next to Janet never stay empty for long. Fortunately, David had the presence of mind to sit down in it before someone else discovered it.

That momentary impulse was to change David's life forever, as well as the lives of the thousands he would inspire with his words. But, a miracle would have to occur first.

I found it hard to believe that the dinner proceeded as if nothing adverse had happened. I watched from across the room as Janet did her work. I knew David was in the very best of hands.

The next day, after the 11:00 AM Sunday service, Janet and I followed the other parishioners out of the door as each shook David's hand. But, before I reached David, Janet took over from where she had left off during dinner the preceding evening.

I went back to the Clinton Chapel and thought my own thoughts. After at least 30 minutes, I returned to rejoin Janet. She and David were still deep in their conversation. All the other parishioners had gone home. I joined Janet and David and we talked for at least another hour.

Janet and I gave assurances that would help to address David's extraordinary needs. We made and met other commitments during the following month.

Shortly after that, we were quite shocked and dismayed when parishioners told Janet and me that David had advised Duck Church that his grief did not allow him to continue in the ministry. As I shook David's hand after the service, I told him that he was obliged to discuss his decision with Janet and me. He agreed to do so.

My regular job as CEO of an important shipyard prepared me to be persuasive in the most challenging of circumstances. I prepared for our discussion with David and knew exactly what words I needed to say which would change his mind and keep him from giving up the ministry. We considered his leaving the ministry to be a significant mistake. I was confident my prepared words would work. Janet would be my witness and supporter.

But, much to my dismay after I started, I realized the words I so carefully had prepared to say to David were not working. I knew David would be lost to the ministry if I gave up. I was on the verge of doing just that.

Then, out of thin air, words came to me that I had neither thought of before nor practiced. As I was receiving these words, I said to David:

"Every word I said to you up to now was carefully planned and practiced. But now I am receiving new words. I am saying them to you as I am receiving them."

As I said these words to David, I knew they came from Michael. I knew they would change David's life forever. The words I received were:

"I am sorry I died."

"But your ministry has always been the part of my life that made me most proud."

"Please don't stop being a minister."

"I will always be alongside you during your life as a minister."

Without my saying anything else, David immediately confirmed that he was sure it was Michael, who was speaking to him through me, because that was exactly what Michael would say. After that, the three of us were speechless and David left.

Later that day, I wrote a letter to David describing what I thought had happened. This letter was his response:

"Dear Rich,

This letter comes to you with deep gratitude. It should have been written sooner but I couldn't find the words to express the emotions I felt after receiving your letter. I still don't have adequate words. I have read it over and over again and I know what you say is true. My initial response was just to weep. There is so much in your letter that speaks to me.

I thank you for caring about my son even though you didn't know him in the flesh. I was going to say that I wish you could have known him but on a very special level you do know him or he knows you. How else could he have spoken to your spirit the words I needed to hear. How else could you perceive that he lives on in me in a deeper sense than just a father son relationship. There is only one other person who has spoken like this ---Libby. She has had some experiences with Michael not for me but for her. It seems that Michael is trying to get to both of us to let us know that everything is all right and that he is more a part of what is going on in our lives than we will ever know.

I find it amusing as well as humbling that God would use you to be the medium through which Michael would speak to me. God is such a wonderful God. Who but God would have chosen an engineer to be a spiritual antenna for the mystery and wonder of Michael's continued life with me. He used an engineer who would not be prone to go off into flights of spiritual wishful thinking to be a spectacular confirmation of a tremendous spiritual truth. And he used the "dead" son of a preacher you really didn't know to take you, the engineer, on a journey beyond your usual analytical world. And then he combined the two worlds together to show that there is no conflict between things of the spirit and things of the mind. Isn't God wonderful?

But I want to make one other point. The blending of the analytical and the spiritual would never have happened if you had not had a heart of love. Your love, concern and compassion for me and Mark were the catalysts that opened the doors.

I thank you for seeing that Michael in his life, in his death and now in his continued life is a gift not only to me but to others. Your appreciation of that gift means more to me than you will ever know. Thank you.

You and Janet have been generous, kind, supportive and wise in every way. As the shadows in my life begin to fade and the hope of the coming sunshine increases I want to thank you for all that you have done for me. You will always be a part of any good I do as a minister of the gospel. For when I wasn't sure if I had anything left to offer, you gave me reason to believe. You were a light in the middle of my stable.

Let me close by saying that you and Janet have been a precious gift to me. A gift that I will always treasure. God knew what he was doing when he sent you into my life. He promised to work for our good in all circumstances. He has kept that promise in my life. He has worked for my good through two rays of light called Rich and Janet. I thank him and you."

Your friend always, David S. Clift

P.S. The wedding has been set for March 24. I hope you will be able to attend! You better than most understand the miracle behind that day.

Several years later, I read a book about Paul the Apostle by Karen Armstrong. It made me think of David so I sent him a second letter. This was David's reply:

From David S. Clift to Rich

Hello Rich,

It was with a great deal of joy that I opened your letter, joy from the simple pleasure of hearing from someone I love and admire, joy because I knew in the letter would be a truth that would make me think and joy because I knew memories would flood back into my mind of a time when Christ fleshed out his love in you and Janet.

I trust that you and Janet are doing well. You are continually in my heart and my prayers. I pray also that the twins are improving and finding better health. It was another movement of God's spirit that your letter came today. I had been called out, as the rescue squad chaplain, last night around 12:30 and didn't get to bed till 3:00 am.

I worked today but came home in the early afternoon and suddenly found myself reliving my separation from Michael. As I have learned to do, I let the renewed grieve surface. I found myself once again praying for contact with Michael as I felt the lost revisited. It has been awhile since the grief returned this hard. After a time of tears and prayer I got up and left the house for a while.

When I returned, there was your package and in it once again a reminder that Michael lives on in my ministry, in my life, in my forever.

Once again, I was reminded of the power of the Spirit in lives receptive to the Spirit's work. Once again you brought to me a message beyond yourself. A message that was needed.

It is wonderful and strange that God would choose an engineer to be a spiritual connection to a hurting pastor. The connection I have with you is not limited by time or space and cannot be explained by any words that I can create. But it is real, it is powerful and it is forever.

God in his grace and love reached down and touched my life with the life of a most unexpected person. I am so pleased that he chose you. I love his sense of humor and creativity. You would have thought he would have used some other pastor or at least a Sunday School teacher. But as you pointed out, who would have expected Paul to be one whom God would use to touch the world with his grace.

I have to smile at the utter uniqueness of God's way of doing things. The Bible says the foolishness of God is wiser than man's wisdom. I have certainly witnessed that truth. I thank him for the intersection of our lives. And I thank you for being open to the Spirit of God in your midst.

I think there is another side to engineer Rich that maybe had not been made alive in your earlier days. It could be, that looking into the pain of a pastor, unlocked a door always there, but not yet opened. Whatever the reason for God's glorious creativity, I am honored to be a part of it. You are a special man.

I thank you for your continued love, your always timely words, your strong encouragement and this time for the gift from Rome. I will find strength in its purpose and inspiration for the motivation that sent it to me. I will read the book with even more interest because it touched your life and caused you to once again look in my direction. You could not have known that it would arrive at a time needed.

I thank God for you and look forward to seeing you sometime soon. October is going to be an outrageously busy month, I have to learn to say no. But if you are going to be in Norfolk during November I would love to drive up and take you out to lunch. It would be a thrill to visit with you. Let me know if there is a time in November that might be possible.

Until the next time, may God bless you and Janet. May he give you a reason to sing and may the light of his love shine brightly on your path.

Your friend always,

David S. Clift"

I suggested to David one day that, while I didn't know any, I was certain that there were individuals listening to his words each Sunday that had experiences similar to his and could benefit from hearing about his feelings and how he managed to cope. David replied that a minister should never burden his parishioners with his own problems.

I responded by saying that life had given him his own set of unique experiences and was it right for him to deny those important experiences that he was most capable of describing from those who might come to him for guidance David was not at all persuaded by my rationale.

But, several weeks later, as he started to give his sermon, I realized he had changed his mind. I listened to his words with much emotion. The others around me seemed to be doing the same. I believed then, and I still believe, it was the most moving sermon I have ever heard.

Several weeks later, David permitted a woman from the congregation to give the sermon. I recognized her as a regular attendee and had heard she was a well-known writer of children's books. I had never spoken to her and knew nothing else about her. She spoke of a young son, who had been the center of her life, but who had died. She spoke of how much she had loved to read books with him when he was alive. She spoke of how she filled the hole in her life caused by her terrible grief and made it through each day by writing books to read to the son she had lost. She spoke of how other children came to enjoy the books she wrote to read to her son.

Maybe the telling of her story to the rest of us helped her get through one more day. Who knows?

There was a small number of others who had lost children who courageously followed her lead to minister to the rest of us by telling their stories. I don't think there was ever anything that brought the members of Duck Church together the way this extraordinary series of lay sermons succeeded in doing.

I think of David often. With Michael's love and encouragement inside of him and powering him, David's ministry greatly expanded the

Duck Church building and congregation Bill Ruth had created.

Because of all that David accomplished afterward, Janet and I believe that the message Michael conveyed to David thru me is one of our most important contributions to the world.

David with Vicki and Rick in Clinton Chapel

I have never stopped wondering how the rules of science I live by as an engineer could have enabled me to receive a message from Michael that seemed to have been transmitted through space and time. Every scientist, including every engineer, knows there is no record of that ever happening.

Human emotions generate human energy. The more intense the emotions, the more human energy is generated. Could it ever be possible for human emotions to become so intense that they could generate the amount of human energy required to transmit human messages through space and time?

Everything I believe as an engineer says no. The only thing that says yes is the fact that Janet, David and I were witnesses when I received the message and conveyed it to David. If it didn't come from Michael, where did it come from?

Sometimes, the spiritual side of me brings me to wonder whether David was right when he sensed a connection between my role as an engineer and Michael's message to him through me.

If-

If you can keep your head when all about you
Others are losing theirs and blaming it on you;
If you can trust yourself when all men doubt you,
But make allowance for their doubting too;
If you can wait and not be tired by waiting,
Or being lied about, don't deal in lies,
Or being hated don't give way to hating,
And yet don't look too good, nor talk too wise:

If you can dream - and not make dreams your master;
If you can think - and not make thoughts your aim,
If you can meet with Triumph and Disaster
And treat those two impostors just the same;
If you can bear to hear the truth you've spoken
Twisted by knaves to make a trap for fools,
Or watch the things you gave your life to, broken,
And stoop and build'em up with worn-out tools:

If you can make one heap of all your winnings
And risk it on one turn of pitch-and-toss,
And lose, and start again at your beginnings
And never breathe a word about your loss;
If you can force your heart and nerve and sinew
To serve your turn long after they are gone,
And so hold on when there is nothing in you
Except the Will which says to them 'Hold on!'

If you can talk with crowds and keep your virtue,
Or walk with Kings - nor lose the common touch,
If neither foes nor loving friends can hurt you,
If all men count with you, but none too much;
If you can fill the unforgiving minute
With sixty seconds' worth of distance run,
Yours is the Earth and everything that's in it,
And - which is more - you'll be a Man, my son!

Rudyard Kipling

EPILOGUE

Until June of this year, I had never been inspired to tell strangers about my life. Then, a rereading of special letters and talks in my files led me to decide that there were words in those special letters and talks that should not die with me.

What Awaits Us?

A week prior to this book being published, I shared words with Dan, one of my thirteen very special Webb classmates. I experienced again the magnificence of relationships between humans that share Planet Earth.

"Dan to Webb Class of 1958 Classmates November 28, 2017

I was hoping I wouldn't have to cross this bridge just yet, but time isn't always on your side. I am now in hospice, although I have no time table. I am doing well, little pain, so far, and a wonderful support system. I have no choice but to acquiesce to what's happening to me, which means I will not be able to make the reunion. I was looking forward to that. Anyway, each of you are invited to visit. I prefer goodbye's to be face to face. I'm not signing off just yet but I suspect it's not very far in the future. My very best to all of you and your families. May the Holidays and New Year be kind to all.

Dan"

Rich to Dan November 28, 2017

"Dear Dan

It seems to me that all creatures have been born mortal for a reason. It also seems to me that, without human mortality, love and friendship would have no value. Because all those I love are mortal, they will always be precious to me. You are one of those who is precious to me and who will remain that way forever.

As we learned as engineers, our existence continues even as the form of our existence changes after life on earth. Having no idea what the next form of that existence might be is the mystery of the universe that most adds to the value we place on our life on earth.

I deeply regret I will not have a chance to honor you and express my friendship and admiration for you at our 60th reunion, as I planned. But, be assured you will be on my mind and part of me as you have been since 1954.

Hospice is a very wise choice. The pain you avoid with Hospice assistance will enable you to extract more value from your remaining days, hours, minutes, seconds and instants.

Farewell my kind and beloved friend and Bon Voyage

Rich"

Dan to Rich November 29, 2017

"Dear Rich, Thank you for your very warm note. What you say certainly has merit and is well considered. My Dad said, just before he passed away, that, "We don't get to make the big decisions." I wish you and Janet the very best of everything. Sixty years is a long time to know someone, although not as long as I would have liked. Even so, I look back at Webb and my classmates with great fondness and respect. Your words are a great source of comfort to me, equaled only by the kindness they convey. I will keep them, and thoughts of you and Janet, in my heart on this journey. Thank you my dear friend.

Dan"

What else is possible?

Not long before reading Dan's news, I awoke earlier than usual one morning at 5:30 AM. An important thought unconsciously came to me which I had never before considered. I got up and wrote it down, just as it came to me. It is:

"The greatness of America's human society seems to be coming to an end.

A diverse handful of ordinary Norfolk, Virginia workers and residents managed to set aside their quests for power and influence over each other and live harmoniously for 25 years.

Is it possible for all of America's humans to do the same?"

ABOUT THE AUTHOR SUMMARY

RICHARD A. GOLDBACH

Metro Machine Corp., Norfolk, VA
CEO from 1977 to 2011
Sole Trustee for ESOP Trust from 1987 to 2011

Ingalls Shipbuilding Div. Litton Industries, Pascagoula, MS.
Project X from 1975 to 1977
Director of Division Planning from 1968 to 1975

Electric Boat Div. General Dynamics, Groton, CT & Quincy, MA
Outfitting & Installation Gen. Superintendent, Quincy from 1965 to 1968
Nuclear Engineering Trainee, Cost Engineer, Asst. Shipwright Supt., Groton 1958 to 1965

Work periods at Brooklyn Naval SY, CDNSWC, U.S. Lines, Bethlehem Steel SY from 1955 to 1958

EDUCATION

Webb Institute of Naval Architecture from 1954 to 1958, BS Naval Arch. & Marine Engr. Degree

PROFESSIONAL

Society of Naval Architects and Marine Engineers (SNAME) member
Chairman of Ship Production Committee
Presented Annual Meeting Paper, "Bid Preparation in Shipbuilding"
Presented Regional Meeting Paper, "Pre-outfitting of AE Ships at Ingalls Shipbuilding
Presented Regional Meeting Paper, "Computer Aided Assists to

Ship Repair"
South Tidewater Association of Ship Repairers-Founder and three-time President
Tidewater Maritime Training Institute-Founder and three-time President
American Society of Naval Engineers

HONORS

Recipient of Webb Institute Selkirk Owen Award for outstanding alumnus of 1999
Awarded Webb Institute Honorary Doctor of Commercial Science Degree in 2014
Recipient of SNAME William M. Kennedy Award for Shipbuilding Systems and Planning

BOARD MEMBERSHIP: Signal Mutual Indemnity Corporation (Workers Compensation)

CIVIC

Chairman-National Maritime Center Authority, Norfolk, VA
Chairman-Chamber of Commerce, Norfolk, VA
District Chairman of Norfolk, VA Boy Scouts of America
President Southside Norfolk Boys & Girls Club
Founder and Administrator of of Metro Machine Elementary School Reading Program

For More Information, Log on to www.shipwrightsuccess.com.

CPSIA information can be obtained
at www.ICGtesting.com
Printed in the USA
FFOW02n0514170118
44593153-44477FF

9 780692 972274